STO

Study Notes

ACP

DISCARDED

P9-ECX-986

DO NOT REMOVE
CARDS FROM POCKET

LIFFS NOTES on

$2.95

SHAW'S MAJOR BARBARA & SAINT JOAN

Cliffs

NOTES INC.

YOUR KEY TO THE CLASSICS

A NOTE TO THE READER

These Notes present a clear discussion of the action and thought of the work under consideration and a concise interpretation of its artistic merits and its significance.

They are intended as a supplementary aid to serious students, freeing them from interminable and distracting note-taking in class. Students may then listen intelligently to what the instructor is saying, and to the class discussion, making selective notes, secure in the knowledge that they have a basic understanding of the work. The Notes are also helpful in preparing for an examination, eliminating the burden of trying to reread the full text under pressure and sorting through class notes to find that which is of central importance.

THESE NOTES ARE NOT A SUBSTITUTE FOR THE TEXT ITSELF OR FOR THE CLASSROOM DISCUSSION OF THE TEXT, AND STUDENTS WHO ATTEMPT TO USE THEM IN THIS WAY ARE DENYING THEMSELVES THE VERY EDUCATION THAT THEY ARE PRESUMABLY GIVING THEIR MOST VITAL YEARS TO ACHIEVE.

These critical evaluations have been prepared by experts who have had many years of experience in teaching the works or who have special knowledge of the texts. They are not, however, incontrovertible. No literary judgments are. There are many interpretations of any great work of literature, and even conflicting views have value for students and teachers, since the aim is not for students to accept unquestionably any one interpretation, but to make their own. The goal of education is not the unquestioning acceptance of any single interpretation, but the development of an individual's critical abilities.

The experience of millions of students over many years has shown that Notes such as these are a valuable educational tool and, properly used, can contribute materially to the great end of literature (to which, by the way, the teaching of literature is itself only a subsidiary)—that is, to the heightening of perception and awareness, the extending of sympathy, and the attainment of maturity by living, in Socrates' famous phrase, "the examined life."

MAJOR BARBARA & SAINT JOAN

NOTES

including

- *Life of the Author*
- *General Plot Summaries*
- *Lists of Characters*
- *Critical Commentaries on Each*
    of the Acts and Scenes
- *Suggested Theme Topics*
- *Selected Bibliography*

by
Jeffery Fisher, M.F.A.
University of Tennessee

INCORPORATED

LINCOLN, NEBRASKA 68501

Editor

Gary Carey, M.A.
University of Colorado

Consulting Editor

James L. Roberts, Ph.D.
Department of English
University of Nebraska

ISBN 0-8220-1154-9
© Copyright 1983
by
C. K. Hillegass
All Rights Reserved
Printed in U.S.A.

Cliffs Notes, Inc.   Lincoln, Nebraska

CONTENTS

MAJOR BARBARA &
SAINT JOAN NOTES

LIFE OF THE AUTHOR

It is with good reason that Archibald Henderson, official biographer of his subject, entitled his work *George Bernard Shaw: Man of the Century*. Well before Shaw's death at the age of ninety-four, this famous dramatist and critic had become an institution. Among the literate, no set of initials were more widely known than G.B.S. Born on July 26, 1856, in Dublin, Ireland, Shaw survived until November 2, 1950. His ninetieth birthday in 1946 was the occasion for an international celebration, the grand old man being presented with a *festschrift*, entitled *GBS 90*, to which many distinguished writers contributed. A London publishing firm bought space in the *Times* to voice its greetings:

GBS

Hail to thee, blithe spirit!

Shaw was the third child and only son in a family which he once described as "shabby but genteel." His father, George Carr Shaw, was employed as a civil servant and later became a not too successful merchant. Shaw remembered especially his father's "alcoholic antics"; the old man was a remorseful, yet an unregenerate drinker. It was from his father that Shaw inherited his superb comic gift. Lucinda Gurley Shaw, the mother, was a gifted singer and music teacher; she led her son to develop a passion for music, particularly operatic music. At an early age, Shaw had memorized many of the works of Mozart, whose fine workmanship he never ceased to admire. Somewhat later, he taught himself to play the piano—in the Shavian manner.

One of the maxims in *The Revolutionist's Handbook*, appended to *Man and Superman*, reads: "He who can, does. He who cannot, teaches." Shaw, who was to insist that all art should be didactic, viewed himself as a kind of teacher, yet he himself had little respect for schoolmasters and formal education. First, his uncle, the Reverend George Carroll, tutored him. Then at the age of ten, Shaw became a pupil at Wesleyan Connexional School in Dublin and later attended two other schools for short periods of time. He hated them all and declared that he had learned absolutely nothing. But Shaw possessed certain qualities which are not always developed in a classroom – for example, an inquisitive mind and a boundless capacity for independent study. Once asked about his early education, he replied: "I can remember no time at which a page of print was not intelligible to me and can only suppose I was born literate." He went on to add that by the age of ten he had saturated himself in the works of Shakespeare and also in the Bible.

A depleted family bank account led Shaw to accept employment as a clerk in a land agency office when he was sixteen. He was unhappy and, determined to become a professional writer, he resigned after five years of service and joined his mother, who was then teaching music in London. The year was 1876. During the next three years, he allowed his mother to support him, and he concentrated largely on trying to support himself as an author. No less than five novels came from his pen between the years 1879 and 1883, but it was soon evident that Shaw's genius would not be fully revealed as a novelist, but as a playwright.

In 1879, Shaw was induced to accept employment in a firm promoting the new Edison telephone, his duties being those of a right-of-way agent. He detested the task of interviewing residents in the East End of London and endeavoring to get their permission for the installation of telephone poles and equipment. A few months of such work was enough for him. In his own words, this was the last time that he "sinned against his nature" by seeking to earn an honest living.

The year 1879 had greater significance for Shaw. He joined the Zetetical Society, a debating club, the members of which held lengthy discussions on such subjects as economics, science, and religion. Soon he found himself in demand as a speaker, and thus he became a regular participant at public meetings. At one such meeting held in September, 1882, he listened spellbound to Henry George, an apostle of Land Nationalization and the Single Tax. Shaw credits the American lecturer and author with having aroused his interest in economics and social theory; previously, Shaw had chiefly concerned himself with the conflict between science and religion. When Shaw was told that no one could do justice to George's theories without being familiar with the theories of Karl Marx, Shaw promptly read a French translation of *Das Kapital*, no English translation then being available. He was immediately converted to socialism.

The year 1884 is also a notable one in the life of Bernard Shaw (as he preferred to be called). After reading a tract entitled *Why Are the Many Poor?* and learning that it was published by the Fabian Society, he appeared at the society's next meeting. The intellectual temper of this group, which included such distinguished men as Havelock Ellis, immediately attracted him. He was accepted as a member on September 5 and was elected to the Executive Committee in January. Among the debaters at Zetetical Society was Sidney Webb, a man whom Shaw recognized as his "natural complement." He easily persuaded Webb to become a Fabian. The two, along with the gifted Mrs. Webb, became the pillars of the society which preached the gospel of constitutional and evolutionary socialism. Shaw's views, voiced in public parks and meeting halls, are expounded at length in *The Intelligent Woman's Guide to Capitalism and Socialism* (1928); many of his ideas also find a place in his dramas.

In the next stage of his career, Shaw emerged as a literary, music, and art critic. Largely because of the influence of William Archer, the distinguished dramatic critic now best remembered as the editor and translator of Ibsen, Shaw became a member of the reviewing staff of the *Pall Mall Gazette* in 1885. Earlier, he had ghostwritten some music reviews for G. L. Lee, with whom his mother had long been associated as a singer and as a music teacher. But this new assignment provided Shaw with his first real experience as a critic. Not long afterward, and again through the assistance of William Archer, Shaw added to these duties those of an art critic on the widely influential *World*. Archer insisted that Shaw knew very little about art but realized that Shaw *thought* that he did—which was what mattered. As for Shaw, he blandly explained that the way to learn about art was to look at pictures; he had begun doing so years earlier in the Dublin National Gallery.

Shaw's close association with William Archer was paramount in his championing the dramas of Henrik Ibsen as new, highly original dramatic works which represented a complete break with the popular theater of the day. "When Ibsen came from Norway," Shaw was to write, "with his characters who thought and discussed as well as acted, the theatrical heaven rolled up like a scroll." Whereas the general public, nurtured on "well-made" romantic and melodramatic plays, denounced Ibsen as a "muck-ferreting dog," Shaw recognized that Ibsen was a great ethical philosopher and a social critic—a role which recommended itself to Shaw immediately. On July 18, 1890, Shaw read a paper on Ibsen at a meeting of the Fabian Society. Amplified, this became *The Quintessence of Ibsen* (1891). Sometimes called *The Quintessence of Shaw*, it sets forth the author's profoundest views on the function of the dramatist, who, Shaw believed, should concern himself foremost with how his characters react to various social forces and who should concern himself further with a new morality based upon an examination and challenge of conventional mores.

In view of what Shaw had written about Ibsen (and about himself) and because of Shaw's dedicated activities as a socialist exhorter, *Widowers' Houses*, his first play, may be called characteristic. Structurally, it represents no departure from the tradition of the well-made play; that is, the action is plotted so that the key situation is exposed in the second act, and the third act is devoted to its resolution. But, thematically, the play was revolutionary in England. It dealt with the evils of slum-landlordism, a subject hardly calculated to regale the typical Victorian audience. Produced at J. T. Grein's Independent Theater in London, it became a sensation because of its "daring" theme, but it was never a theatrical success. Shaw, however, was not at all discouraged. The furor delighted him. No one knew better than he the value of attracting attention. He was already at work on *The Philanderer*, an amusing but rather slight comedy of manners.

In 1894, Shaw's *Arms and the Man* enjoyed a good run at the Avenue Theater from April 21 to July 7, and it has been revived from time to time to this very day. At last, the real Shaw had emerged—the dramatist who united irrepressible gaiety and complete seriousness of purpose. The play has been described as "a satire on the prevailing bravura style," and it sets forth the "view of romance as the great heresy to be swept from art and life."

In the same year, Shaw wrote *Mrs. Warren's Profession*, which became a *cause célèbre*. Shaw himself grouped it with his so-called "Unpleasant Plays." Dealing with the economic causes of prostitution and the conflict between the prostitute mother and her daughter, it created a tumult which was kept alive for several years on both sides of the Atlantic. It may well be argued that in this play, Shaw was far more the polemicist than the artist, but the play still has its place among the provocative dramas of ideas.

The indefatigable Shaw was already at work on his first unquestionably superior play, *Candida*. First produced in 1895, it has been popular ever since and has found its place in anthologies. Notable for effective character portrayal and the adroit use of inversions, it tells how Candida and the Reverend Morell, widely in public demand as an advanced thinker, reached an honest and sound basis for a lasting marriage.

While working with the Fabians, Shaw met the personable Charlotte Payne-Townshend, an Irish heiress deeply concerned with the many problems of social justice. He was immediately attracted to her. After she had helped him through a long illness, the two were married in 1898, and she became his modest but capable critic and assistant throughout the years of their marriage.

During this period, there was no surcease of playwriting on Shaw's part. He completed *You Never Can Tell, The Man of Destiny*, and *The Devil's Disciple*. This last play, an inverted Victorian-type melodrama was first acted in the United States, where it was an immediate success, financially and otherwise. By the turn of the century, Shaw had written *Caesar and Cleopatra* and *The Admirable Bashville*. He was now the acknowledged major force in the new drama of the twentieth century.

The year 1903 is especially memorable for the completion and publication of *Man and Superman*. It was first acted (without the *Don Juan In Hell* intermezzo, which constitutes Act III) in 1905. Then, some twenty-three other plays were added to the Shavian canon as the century advanced toward the halfway mark. Best known among these are *Major Barbara* (1905), *Androcles and the Lion* (1912), *Pygmalion* (1913), *Heartbreak House* (1919), *Back to Methuselah* (1920), and *Saint Joan* (1923). During the years 1930-32, the Ayot St. Lawrence Edition of his collected plays was published. Shaw's literary preeminence had found world-wide recognition. He refused, however, to accept either a knighthood or the Order of Merit offered by the Crown, but in 1926 he did accept the Nobel Prize for Literature. It was quite typical of him to state that the award was given to him by a grateful public because he had not published anything during that year.

Shaw persistently rejected offers from film makers. According to one story, when importuned by Samuel Goldwyn, the well-known

Hollywood producer, he replied: "The difficulty, Mr. Goldwyn, is that you are an artist and I am a businessman." Later, however, the ardor and ability of Gabriel Pascal impressed him, and Shaw agreed to prepare the scenario of *Pygmalion* for production. The film, released in 1938, was a notable success. *Major Barbara* and *Androcles and the Lion* followed, and the Irish-born dramatist had now won a much larger audience. *My Fair Lady*, a musical adapted from *Pygmalion*, opened in New Haven, Connecticut, on February 4, 1956, starring Rex Harrison and Julie Andrews, and it was and remains a spectacular success. A film version won an Academy Award in 1964 as Best Picture.

Discussing *Macbeth*, Shaw once wrote: "I want to be thoroughly used up when I die, for the harder I work, the more I live. I rejoice in life for its own sake. Life is no 'brief candle' for me. It is a sort of splendid torch, which I have got hold of for the moment; and I want to make it burn as brightly as possible before handing it on to future generations." Life indeed was a bright torch which burned long for Bernard Shaw. Almost to the very end, although he was bedridden with a broken hip, he lived up to his credo. He was ninety-two years old in 1949, when *Buoyant Billions* was produced at the Malvern Festival. In the same year, his highly readable *Sixteen Self Sketches* was published. He was planning on writing still another play when he died on November 2, 1950.

MAJOR BARBARA NOTES

GENERAL PLOT SUMMARY

Lady Britomart has summoned her twenty-four-year-old son, Stephen, into the drawing room to discuss the family's finances for the first time in Stephen's life. It seems that both of his sisters are about to be married and both young women need extra money. While the younger, Sarah, is marrying into money, her fiancé, Charles Lomax, won't come into his millions until he is thirty-five years old. Barbara, the older sister, has abandoned all social pretension and has entered into a life of service in the Salvation Army, where she holds the rank of Major. Major Barbara has also attracted the attentions of a Professor of Greek who has joined the Salvation Army in order to be near Major Barbara; unfortunately, he is "poor as a church mouse." Furthermore, it is time that Stephen think of marrying. Consequently, Lady Britomart has summoned her former husband, the immensely wealthy Andrew Undershaft, to come that evening to meet his family with the idea of obtaining additional monies from him for each of the children.

Lady Britomart then sends for her daughters and their fiancés, Charles Lomax and Professor Adolphus Cusins. When the daughters hear that their father is due to arrive at any minute, there is some alarm until Major Barbara announces that *even her father* has a soul and that his soul *needs* to be saved!

When Undershaft is announced, he is confused about the identities of everyone present until Cusins takes charge of matters and straightens things out. Undershaft then shows an immediate interest in Major Barbara's work for the Salvation Army, and he maintains that there are many similarities between the Salvation Army and his own munitions factory. After a lengthy discussion about the morals of both organizations, Major Barbara and her father make a bargain to visit each other's places; tomorrow, he will come to her shelter, and she, in turn, will visit his munitions factory. To settle the agreement, the family, along with the fiancés, decides to sing the rousing, militant Salvation Army tune "Onward Christian Soldiers."

The next day at the Salvation Army Shelter, two frequenters of the Shelter are talking: Rummy Mitchens reveals to Snobby Price that she, Rummy, is merely pretending to be a worse sinner than she is because "the lasses" at the Shelter like it better. Snobby then reveals that *his* act is also fraudulent, composed only of "made up stories." At this moment, young Jenny Hill, eighteen years old, arrives with Peter Shirley, a middle-aged man who desires to work but who cannot find a job. Suddenly, a tough young man named Bill Walker bursts into the Shelter demanding the whereabouts of his girlfriend and accuses the Salvation Army of separating them. Then, without warning, Bill strikes Jenny in the jaw. Peter and Rummy try to separate the two, Snobby cowers cowardly in front of the bully, Rummy is knocked down, but Shirley stands his ground, and he challenges Walker to fight Todger Fairmile, a wrestler and a new convert to the Salvation Army. At this point, Major Barbara arrives and takes down

Shirley's name; when she approaches Walker, however, he refuses to give her his name. Thus, she writes that he is the "man who struck Jenny Hill." After further conversation with Walker, and just as Major Barbara is on the verge of discovering that this ruffian also has a conscience, Cusins arrives with Andrew Undershaft, and Barbara tells Cusins to explain to her father how the Shelter functions; then she goes into the Shelter to attend to business.

In a discussion about the nature of religion and various virtues of truth, honor, and justice as contrasted with Undershaft's money and power, Cusins maintains that Undershaft will have to choose between Barbara's views and Undershaft's own unique views. Cusins's frankness and his understanding of religion appeal to Undershaft, as does Undershaft's ironic and paradoxical sense of life appeal to Cusins. When Cusins points out Major Barbara's devotion to the common man, then Undershaft, who was born and grew up in poverty, points out that a love of poverty (and thus dirt, disease, and suffering) is unnatural. He asserts that he, Cusins, and Barbara are "above" the common people, and therefore they have an obligation to work together to elevate the common people. To do so and since he cannot "buy" Barbara, he must buy the Salvation Army.

Suddenly, at this moment, the members of the Shelter return from one of their fund raising meetings. After the money is counted, and the sum is discovered to be short a few pence, Undershaft offers to make up the difference, but Major Barbara refuses, telling her father that he cannot "buy" his salvation. Bill Walker then returns after an encounter with Todger Fairmile, and he says that he wants to make a contribution as amends for hurting Jenny Hill, but again, Major Barbara asserts that the Salvation Army *cannot* be bought. At this point, Mrs. Baines, a Salvation Army commissioner, arrives and meets Undershaft. She enthusiastically describes the work of the Salvation Army (explaining that the Army feeds the poor enough so that they won't strike against the capitalists), and she ecstatically tells about an offer made to the Army by a man named Bodger, England's chief manufacturer of gin and beer. Bodger, she says, has offered 5,000 pounds to the Army if a donor, or donors, can be found to match this sum of money. Undershaft gladly writes out a check for this sum to the utter horror of Barbara and to the cynical amazement of Bill Walker, who asks Barbara, "What price salvation now?"

When Major Barbara protests that the Army cannot accept questionable or "tainted" money, she is barraged with a series of seductive arguments in favor of accepting the money. Cusins begins preparing for a parade to announce that the Shelters *will* remain open, and Major Barbara quietly removes her badge of office and pins it on her father. As most of the others march out, Bill Walker becomes angered that the money which Barbara refused to take from him has now been stolen by Snobby Price. When Major Barbara offers to refund him his money, he in turn tells her that *he* will not be "bought." After Bill leaves, Peter Shirley and Barbara leave, consoling one another.

The next day, in Lady Britomart's drawing room, Cusins enters in a drunken state announcing that the Salvation Army's rally was a great success and that afterward he spent the night drinking Spanish burgundy with Undershaft. Shortly afterward, Undershaft arrives to settle money matters with Lady Britomart. He readily concedes to the demands which she makes for Barbara and Sarah, but he is adamant in his intention to leave the remainder of his fortune to a foundling, keeping the tradition of the Undershaft Munitions — that it, the factory must *always* be left to a foundling. Undershaft, however, does agree to help Stephen get started in a good job, and after a lengthy discussion with Lady Britomart, they decide that Stephen would be a good journalist because he knows how to use words that have no meaning. When the others return, Undershaft reminds Barbara that it is now time for her to keep her part of the bargain and visit the munitions factory. As they all leave, Barbara braces herself to see an eternal pit of fire and damnation — in short, a "factory of death."

Upon arriving at the munitions village, the Undershafts and fiancés are astonished to find that it is a model of absolute perfection — it is marred only by the fact that everyone lives there with the knowledge that they might "be blown to smithereens at any moment." In a discussion of the Undershaft tradition of having a foundling inherit the entire fortune and the factory, Cusins reveals that through a technicality (his mother — Cusins's mother — was his father's dead wife's sister, which makes Cusins illegitimate in England, even though he was considered legitimate in Australia, where he was born), he is *legally* a foundling — but he does not know, really, if he wants the job *or* the inheritance. Cusins has no qualms about changing his name, but he is totally opposed to war and destruction. Undershaft then cleverly points out that cannons do not kill men – it is the men who fire the cannons that kill men. He challenges Cusins to take the job and then use his money and power to change human nature – to create men of honesty and courage and moral conviction. Undershaft then leaves Cusins and Barbara together, and they both agree that they could use the munitions factory for the benefit of mankind and, furthermore, that Barbara, instead of converting people by promising them food and shelter, would now be able to convert people who are in no dire need of physical comforts. Thus, once again, after leaving the Army, Barbara "returns to her colors."

LIST OF CHARACTERS

Andrew Undershaft

Even though the play is entitled *Major Barbara*, Andrew Undershaft is the dominant figure of the play, and he is also Shaw's ironic spokesman, especially when Undershaft advocates that peace can best be achieved by the manufacture of munitions and arms of all sorts, that poverty is the worst of all crimes, as well as when he says that charity only contributes to poverty, that all money is tainted – meaning that none is – that sufficient money is better than a good conscience, that only a successful capitalist can actually afford to build the perfect socialistic society, and that a creator of destruction is necessary for the creator of a new social structure.

Major Barbara

One of Undershaft's daughters; at first, she is a Major in the Salvation Army, intent upon converting souls by providing them with bread and treacle, but she changes from being militant about the "rightness" of her religious organization in order to become a part of her father's munitions factory's ideal town, a town where people are already well fed and clothed and, thus, they are not in materialistically dire straits as well as in spiritual distress. In this setting, she can practice her work of "saving souls" without having to deal with "free loaders."

Lady Britomart

The estranged wife of Andrew Undershaft; as her name suggests, Lady Britomart is the epitome of the sterile upper class of Britain which is concerned with the usefulness of money and with maintaining the proper social decorum.

Stephen Undershaft

The rather innocuous, if not inept, son of Andrew Undershaft and Lady Britomart. His lack of finances and general incompetence is the impetus for the beginning of the play since Andrew Undershaft is about to disinherit him and leave the Undershaft fortune to a foundling, in keeping with the long tradition of always leaving the inheritance to a competent foundling rather than trust in the incompetence of family.

Adolphus Cusins

Major Barbara's fiancé and a scholar of Greek language and literature; he has a highly imaginative and intellectual mind. There are a rather contrived series of events concerning his birth, making him technically an orphan (or foundling) — that is, technically, he is legitimate in Australia where he was born, but in Britain, he is considered to be a foundling because his mother was his father's wife's sister, a relationship that was not legally recognized in England; thus, as a foundling, he will become the next head of the Undershaft Munitions Foundry.

Charles Lomax

Sarah's rather silly fiancé; he is constantly making stinging and ironic remarks. In contrast to Lady Britomart's views and in support of Andrew Undershaft's views, he illustrates perfectly that the "aristocracy" is not fit to run *any* type of business.

Morrison

Lady Britomart's butler and an old retainer who was in service to the household before Lady Britomart and Andrew Undershaft separated; he is somewhat confused as to how to announce the sudden arrival of his old master. His confusion thus provides some basic comic relief.

Bill Walker

A ruffian who bullies everyone in the Salvation Army Shelter; when he tries to "buy" forgiveness and atonement, his contribution of only a sovereign (about five dollars then) is rejected. This contrasts with the fact that while the Army rejects *his* small contribution, it is quite willing to accept the larger contribution (5,000 pounds – about 25,000 dollars) from a brewer and a munitions maker, Bodger and Undershaft. Bill Walker's utterance ("What price salvation now?") becomes a central comment on the nature of the Salvation Army and its ethics in accepting money from any source.

Mrs. Baines

A rather high officer in the Salvation Army, she is in charge of raising money for the Army. Unlike Major Barbara, she sees no contradiction or violation of the principles of the Army in accepting money that some people (Major Barbara, for example) consider to be "tainted." Her point of view is that the wealthy Bodger does not *force* poor people to buy his gin and beer and therefore his money is as good as any because, along with Undershaft's contribution, these monies will allow the Shelters to remain open for the benefit of the poor during the forthcoming winter. Without these contributions, thousands of poor people would have no place to turn for food or shelter. Thus, Miss Baines represents the practical aspects of the Salvation Army. She is a realist who understands the importance of money without questioning its source.

Jenny Hill

Seemingly, Snobby is a rather permanent fixture at the Salvation Army Shelter. He represents the hypocrite who lies in order to gain attention and who is willing to publicly acclaim his sins (he swears, for example, that he beats his poor old mother all the time) in order to help the Army collect money from those who are touched by his "heartbreaking confessions."

Rummy Mitchens

Another fraudulent, hypocritical convert; she is an older woman who enjoys the attention that the young "lasses" at the Shelter heap upon her because of the numerous and lurid "sins" that she is able to vividly narrate.

Peter Shirley

Peter is a forty-six-year-old man who has been discharged from his job because he is too old. He is too proud to accept charity, and he strongly desires to find legitimate employment. He is both an ardent Secularist (as is Andrew Undershaft, we think!), and he is also anti-capitalistic, even though at the end of the play, he acepts a job at the Undershaft Munitions Factory. When Peter first meets Andrew Undershaft, an often-quoted witty exchange occurs between the two men: Shirley tells Undershaft, "I wouldn't have your conscience, not for all your income" and Undershaft replies, "I wouldn't have your income, not for all your conscience."

Bilton

The foreman at the munitions foundry who refuses to allow anyone to have matches. This is a humorous way of reminding everyone that they are liable to be "blown to smithereens" at any moment.

Mog Habbijem and Todger Fairmile

These two characters never appear in the drama but they are often referred to. Mog Habbijem is the person whom Bill Walker is looking for because he is furious with the Salvation Army for converting her. Todger Fairmile is the expert wrestler (and therefore extremely strong) who is now Mog's boyfriend and, as we hear later, he does not fight with Bill Walker but merely pins him down in an attempt to convert him. While this scene is only narrated in the drama, those who have seen the famous movie (1940) will remember that the skirmish scene was actually included.

SHAW'S PREFACE TO *MAJOR BARBARA*

In many of his plays, Shaw writes a preface for the reader which, in some cases, has very little to do with the play itself, but, in some cases, as with *Major Barbara*, it comments directly on the ideas found in the play. And as with this play, the prefaces are often rather lengthy and are divided into sections.

In the first section of this preface, entitled "First Aid to Critics," Shaw attacks one of his favorite groups of adversaries – those critics who sought to prove that he had no originality in his ideas and, furthermore, that his ideas were thinly disguised imitations of foreign philosophies, and those who said that Shaw was only "echoing Schopenhauer, Nietzsche, Ibsen. . . ." Instead, Shaw maintains in the Preface that he is influenced much more by writers native to the British Isles than by foreign writers, and he cites such authors as Charles Lever, and such groups as the Fabian Socialists. Furthermore, the themes used in this play are themes that he has already used: (1) the conflict between reality and romantic posturing (see CLIFFS NOTES' *Arms and the Man*); (2) the presentation of a woman (Major Barbara) as an independent person rather than a toy (or plaything) of men, as was seen in Shaw's *Man and Superman*; as was also (3) the idea of the superman (Undershaft and Cusins) as the savior of society.

Second, in "The Gospel of St. Andrew Undershaft," Shaw reinforces Undershaft's position that poverty is the greatest of all evils and the worst of all crimes. Here, Shaw is using evil and crime in a different sense from that of the average reader's understanding of the words. Shaw would defend a theft which a poor working man might commit – that is, if he were likely to have "to see his children starve whilst idle people over-feed pet dogs." This type of unfair distribution of wealth leads, naturally, according to Shaw, to various types of justifiable crimes. Shaw wants not only "legal minimum wages" and "old age pensions," but he also advocates "universal pensions for life." That is, Shaw believes in the redistribution of wealth so that no man need go hungry or be in want. If he receives money from the government, he should also be provided some sort of work so as to *earn* that money. He ultimately suggests that all poverty should be illegal. In a perfect society, money is the most important thing; "it represents health, strength, honor, generosity, and beauty." When poverty is eradicated, the morals of a nation will naturally be taken care of.

In the third section, "The Salvation Army," Shaw seems to be having fun needling the critics who do not know how to respond properly to his use of the Salvation Army. Whereas some critics have accused him of attacking the Salvation Army, Shaw maintains that even the Army itself understands perfectly well the necessity of taking "tainted" money in order to continue its operations. In fact, it rings somewhat false that Major Barbara ever refused the money in the first place.

In "Barbara's Return to the Colors," Shaw maintains that there is something basically appealing about substituting a drum for the organ, as did the Salvationists when they went about marching through the streets instead of merely sitting and praying. Ultimately, Barbara must learn that bribing people to salvation through "bread and treacle" is not as noble as is converting people to their own accord. At least it is to be hoped that Barbara's knowledge "will clearly lead to something more hopeful than distributing bread and treacle at the expense of Bodger."

In the next section, "The Weaknesses of the Salvation Army," Shaw acknowledges that the Army, at present, is building a worthy and efficient "business organization," but he feels compelled to point out some of its weaknesses. Basically, he says, there is still "too much other-worldliness about the Army." That is, the Army emphasizes that salvation exists in the next world, whereas Shaw wants to correct poverty and injustice in *this* world, immediately. The Army encourages the "nasty lying habit called confession." Shaw thoroughly dislikes any system that allows confession as atonement for sin (crime) because confession will allow the offender to feel free to commit the same offense again. Finally, the Army, instead of coddling the poor, should be encouraging them to stand up and demand their rights.

In "Christianity and Anarchism," Shaw refers to a recent international event (a royal wedding followed by a bullfight and an explosion) in which demands were made that cruel punishment be meted out to the offending rebels. For Shaw, this is not Christianity, but "Crosstianity"; it is pure vengeance disguised under the cloak of Christianity. Instead, for the church to be true to itself, it should not conspire with the state to keep "the poor in their places" but, instead, it should emphasize a true sense of equality and brotherhood among people.

In "Sane Conclusions," Shaw reemphasizes some of his points. First, every able-bodied man must be expected and allowed to work and to earn money commensurate with his efforts. The wealth of the nation should be in proportion to the efforts of the workers; and second, all harsh, unusual, and cruel punishments should be abolished. Such punishments waste manpower that could be put to better uses. Next, Shaw maintains that there should be talk of atonement: "A man's deeds are irrevocable," and he must be held responsible for them. A man's life is to be measured in relationship to his usefulness to society. Finally, Shaw urges all institutions, especially the church and the Salvation Army, to become intellectually honest—to recognize true "mischief" for what it is and not to offer atonement and not allow an offender to be redeemed by mere expressions of repentance and confession.

CRITICAL COMMENTARIES

ACT I *(The opening scene between Stephen Undershaft and his mother, Lady Britomart)*

Summary

The play begins when the estranged wife of Andrew Undershaft, Lady Britomart, calls Stephen, her son, in for a conference. Lady Britomart is so domineering and Stephen is so intimidated that he is virtually speechless. She immediately corrects his behavior, reminds him that he is now twenty-four years old and thus a grown man, and that he has traveled throughout most of the world; therefore, it is now time that he take over some of the responsibilities of conducting the family's business affairs. Stephen becomes increasingly more intimidated by his mother and maintains that he has deliberately avoided entering into the family's affairs. Stephen, out of respect for his mother's feelings, has been especially reluctant to mention his father's name; Stephen's father, however, is *exactly* the topic that Lady Britomart wants to discuss. She says, "We can't go on all our lives not mentioning him." She then begins to lay out the problems facing them and the necessity for talking about Stephen's father, Andrew Undershaft, the fabulously wealthy munitions manufacturer who has not seen any of his family since the children were very small.

As Lady Britomart outlines the "family problem," we learn that Stephen's two sisters are planning on marriage. Sarah Undershaft has made a good match, but her fiancé cannot come into his millions until he is thirty-five years old. In the meantime, the couple will have to have more than his present eight-hundred-a-year allowance in order to live in the manner to which they are accustomed. Even worse, Barbara Undershaft, who showed such promise of making a brilliant match, has, instead, joined the Salvation Army, and she spends her evenings with a "professor of Greek," whom, according to Lady Britomart, Barbara "picked up in the street" and who pretends to be a Salvationist and plays the big Army drum for Barbara in public because he has "fallen head over ears in love with her." Lady Britomart, however, maintains – indeed, she *insists* – that she herself is not a snob; therefore, a professor of Greek will make a respectable and present-able husband because no one objects to classical Greek, but this pair will *also* need money because professors are notoriously as "poor as church mice." And, furthermore, it is a known "fact," according to Lady Britomart, that refined, poetic people like Adolphus Cusins need more money than other people do because they are too esoteric to under-stand money; thus, they will need a large sum of money for their mar-riage. Finally, Lady Britomart tells Stephen that she expects *him* to get married soon; he has been a bachelor long enough.

With the above explanations and with the knowledge that Lady Britomart's father, the Earl of Stevenage, needs all of his resources to keep up his position in society, she wonders: where *is* the money to come from? She then points out to Stephen that because there is always a war going on *somewhere*, Stephen's father surely must be fabulously wealthy. Stephen agrees and points out how well-known the Undershaft name is and how he has been the victim of many unpleasant comments because his name is associated with the "blood and destruction" of the Undershaft munitions. In fact, they both agree, the firm of Undershaft and Lazarus controls most of the munitions of Europe (if not of most of the world), and it is beyond the arm of the law; thus, Andrew has used his power to establish his own ec-centric concepts of morals and ethics. Here, it is important to note that Lady Britomart explains that she left Andrew Undershaft because he became head of the Undershaft corporations for one reason only – because he was not a *legal* heir: he was illegitimate, a foundling – and it has been a centuries-old tradition to leave the business to *another* foundling. Therefore, Lady Britomart became highly indignant when Andrew insisted that he would leave his wealth to another foundling rather than to his natural son, Stephen. Furthermore, while Andrew has lived a perfectly moral life himself, he has nevertheless advocated things that his wife considers immoral: "So I couldn't forgive Andrew for preaching immorality while he practiced morality." Therefore, she left Andrew to protect the children from his outrageous and unconventional morals and opinions. However, they have always been dependent on him financially, and even though Stephen is naively shocked to hear his mother speak so boldly, Lady Britomart points out that she has asked Undershaft to come here this very evening to discuss the financial arrangements which will be necessary for the marriages. Thus, Undershaft is due to arrive any minute. This impending appearance, as might be expected, causes further dismay for Stephen.

Commentary

This first scene conventionally and economically sets up some of the main conflicts in the drama; that is, we learn *who* is to inherit the munitions factory and the facts about Andrew Undershaft's immense wealth. In traditional dramatic terms, this scene would be called "the exposition scene"; Shaw's technique is influenced by the famous Norwegian dramatist Henrik Ibsen, whom Shaw admired and wrote about (see Shaw's *The Quintessence of Ibsenism*). "Exposition" means, basically, presenting those matters which inform the audience about the situation of the play and explain the main issues that are to become the central core of the drama. Thus, the play opens with a confrontation between a mother and her son, and through their conversation, we learn a great deal. For example, the entire conversation takes place because of the necessity of arranging financial support for Stephen's two sisters, and therefore the subject of Stephen's and his sisters' father must be brought up. This, in turn, allows the audience to know that the father's name has *never* been discussed by Lady Britomart and her children; thus, the topic is a highly embarrassing one for her son.

While Shaw is technically presenting his audience with the necessary background information for the drama which is to follow, he is also able, at the same time, to entertain his audience by playing up the conflict and the contrast between mother and son. Lady Britomart is a marvelous character; she is liberal enough to accept other peoples' opinions, but only if they agree with her preconceived ideas. She adores advice from her son, but only if it is the formulation of a course of action which *she* has already planned.

As her name implies, Lady Britomart is the epitome of everything that is *British*. In a classic work of early English literature, Spenser's *Faerie Queene*, one of the central characters is Britomart, a female knight, symbolizing militant chastity; thus, Lady Britomart becomes Shaw's symbol of militant upper-class English morality. She has been exasperated with her husband – not for anything *immoral* that he has done, but simply for the reason that he will not conform to what she considers to be the "proper" behavior for a person in his position. After all, he has proposed to disinherit his son in favor of a *foundling*, someone whom he has not even discovered yet – and all for the sake of a principle. Lady Britomart, in contrast, stands firmly within the philosophy of the English aristocracy, assured that no foundling can possess the qualities that a member of a noble family can have; her son is, after all, the grandson of a English Earl, and yet while espousing these views, Lady Britomart is able to caustically castigate her future son-in-law, Charles Lomax, a member of the nobility, because of his basic incompetence. In fact, it is Charles Lomax's incompetence and his inability to earn money that makes it necessary to call upon Undershaft for future financial aid. Furthermore, Lady Britomart sees no discrepancy between disapproving of Undershaft and the manner in which he makes money and the fact that she has been completely dependent upon his money throughout all of these years. Even her son Stephen is shocked to realize that all of their present income comes from Andrew Undershaft. Consequently, this conflict between the family's reliance upon this money for their existence introduces one of the main themes of the drama – that is, the domestic dilemma will later be correlated with the dilemma of the Salvation Army when the Army will, finally, decide to gladly accept "tainted" money from "tainted" sources in order to insure its continued existence, and then it will pray for the "tainted" people who donated the money. Consequently, the domestic dilemma introduced in this first scene parallels one of the central themes of the drama.

This scene also prepares us for the appearance of other characters. Even though Lady Britomart is sharply opinionated, we are ready to accept her evaluations of some of the other characters. Later, we see that her future son-in-law, Charles Lomax, has been described by her in perfect terms; he is, indeed, something of a "noodle" – a rather fashionable but incompetent member of the aristocracy. Likewise, she snobbishly approves of having a scholar of Greek literature as a son-in-law, but she is also very practical and knows that one cannot live on prestige and snobbery. Consequently, she has undertaken the practical steps of calling her former husband to meet his family for the sole purpose of getting additional commitments for financial support for their children.

ACT I *(The brief scene between the family, just prior to the arrival of Andrew Undershaft)*

Summary

Having prepared Stephen for the arrival of his father, Lady Britomart now sends Morrison, the butler, to fetch her daughters and their respective fiancés so that they might be told of the imminent arrival of Undershaft. Barbara and Sarah arrive first, Barbara dressed in her major's uniform from the Salvation Army and Sarah dressed in the fashionable attire of the time. Sarah is dumbfounded when she hears her mother's news, and her fiancé, Charles Lomax, makes a few inappropriate, fatuous remarks, greatly to the chagrin of Lady Britomart. Barbara, in contrast, will be glad to see her father since he "has a soul to be saved like anybody else." Adolphus Cusins (Dolly) makes some more humorous and subtle quips, but he speaks Lady Britomart's mind when he says that they should *all* behave themselves because their conduct is a reflection upon how Lady Britomart has brought up the children.

Commentary

This brief transitional scene serves chiefly to introduce us to the other main characters and to give Andrew Undershaft time to arrive upon the scene. Since Shaw, as a dramatist, spends considerable effort writing for the *readers* of his plays, it is important to note his descriptions of the characters. In a key description, for example, he is careful to differentiate between the two sisters: Sarah is "slender, bored and mundane" and dressed fashionably, whereas Barbara is the more livelier, wittier, and jollier of the two; she is the energetic sister. Likewise, the two fiancés are also clearly delineated: Charles Lomax is simply content to be a young man-about-town, possessing a rather flippant or frivolous sense of humor which brings Lady Britomart often to the brink of despair. Cusins, however, has an intellectual detachment, and if we know now that at the end of the drama, he will be selected to take charge of the Undershaft and Lazarus Munitions factories, we will see how thoroughly qualified he is for that position, even in Shaw's early description of him. For example, Shaw writes: "He is a most implacable, determined, tenacious, intolerant person who . . . is considerate, gentle, explanatory, even mild and apologetic, capable possibly of murder, but not of cruelty or coarseness." These seemingly contradictory qualities will, therefore, make him a highly qualified person to manage the very humane, yet very destructive company of Lazarus and Undershaft Munitions.

ACT I *(Andrew Undershaft meets his family)*

Summary

Morrison, the butler, announces the arrival of Andrew Undershaft, who is an "easy-going elderly man, with kindly patient manners, and an engaging simplicity of character . . . but he has . . . formidable reserves of power, both bodily and mental." Undershaft greets his wife courteously and graciously. Lady Britomart makes a sweeping gesture and tells him: "This is your family." At first, Undershaft is confused that he has such a large family, and he initially mistakes Lomax for his son, and then he thinks that Stephen is a stranger named "Mr. Stephen"; when he turns to Adolphus Cusins, Cusins, with his scholarly correctness, takes charge of matters and sets Undershaft straight by identifying everyone present in their correct relationship to him.

As they settle themselves, Undershaft admits how uncomfortable he is because "if I play the part of a father, I shall produce the effect of an intrusive stranger; and if I play the part of a discreet stranger, I may appear a callous father." After a number of awkward pauses in the conversation, the subject of Barbara's involvement in the Salvation Army is brought up. Undershaft indicates a great interest in Barbara's work, particularly in the Salvation Army's use of militant and military music to win converts. He also feels an affinity for the motto of the Salvation Army: "Blood and Fire"; this very motto might well serve his own munitions company as well as it serves the Army — and, after all, they both, father and daughter, *do* serve some sort of Army. Barbara provides souls for *her* Army, and Undershaft provides arms for *his* armies. Undershaft furthermore maintains that his "sort of blood cleanses; my sort of fire purifies."

When Lomax suggests that even though cannons might be necessary, one still can't approve of them, Undershaft doesn't mind such criticism because he is in a good mood; this morning, his foundry perfected a gun with which the testers could blow "twenty-seven dummy soldiers into fragments . . . [a gun] which formerly destroyed only thirteen." Undershaft further explains that he is not ashamed of his profession; he does not keep his "morals and [his] business in watertight compartments." Unlike other people who make immense sums of questionable money and then give large sums to hospitals, churches, and other organizations as conscience money, he uses his profits in order to experiment and create better weapons and research "in improved methods of destroying life and property." True Christianity, with its philosophy of turning the other cheek, would make him bankrupt. His own morality, therefore, must have a place in it for cannons and torpedoes.

In a further discussion of what constitutes true morality, Barbara argues with her father; she says that from her experience, there are no really good or evil men in the world – only sinners – and that "the same salvation [is] ready for them all," regardless of social rank or profession. This leads Undershaft to wonder if Barbara has ever "saved" anyone in the munitions profession. Thus, they strike a good bargain with each other: he challenges Barbara that if he comes to her Salvation Army Shelter, would she come to his munitions factory the next day, and, afterward, they can compare the quality of life found in both places. He then wonders, aloud, which one of them will convert the other. As they agree to the joint visits, Barbara says that her Shelter will be found at the sign of the *cross*, and Undershaft says that his foundry is located at the sign of the *sword*. To solidify the agreement, Barbara decides to ask Lomax to play "Onward Christian Soldiers," but Lady Britomart is offended and announces that if there is to be a religious observance, it will have to be done properly, with the Anglican prayer book, but the others ignore her and go into the drawing room for a service featuring the loud music of the Salvation Army's tambourine and concertina.

Left alone with Cusins, Sarah, and Stephen, Lady Britomart tells Cusins that she knows that the only reason that he joined the Salvation Army was to be with Barbara, and thereupon Cusins playfully asks her not to tell on him. She then sends Sarah out to join the others and bemoans to her son Stephen how unjust it is for her to have to shoulder the problems of bringing up the children only to have the children completely attracted to their father when they are grown.

Commentary

This scene sets up the essential conflict in the drama – that is, the conflict between Major Barbara's view of life, contrasted with the view of life expressed by her father, Andrew Undershaft. But before this serious conflict is presented, it is echoed in a minor sort of way by the appearance of Undershaft, who has not seen his family for many years even though he has been their financial mainstay of support during all these years. The case of the father mistakenly identifying his children provides the traditional comedy required in this scene. On a serious level, however, this is a wry comment on the fact that Undershaft will indeed adopt a foundling to run the munitions factory, and it is a prelude to the fact that he will disinherit his own son, who is seen here and elsewhere as a simp, incapable of running such a huge operation; this matter is humorously treated though, as Undershaft mistakes, first, Lomax for his son, then rejects his son Stephen as a stranger, someone named "Mr. Stephen," and then Undershaft turns to Adolphus Cusins as his real son. This is ironic since at the end of the play it will be Adolphus who will become the next heir to the munitions factories. Cusins is the only person in the midst of all this confusion to have the presence of mind to straighten things out for Andrew Undershaft, and this indebts him already to Undershaft.

Undershaft, throughout the scene, is a person of rather commanding appearance and personality. He is intellectually agile and, apparently, he has the advantage of being old enough to have worked out his own views towards religion and morality. He does not believe in the Christian motto which enjoins people not to resist evil. To follow the Christian doctrine and submit to evil would mean the destruction of his entire munitions empire. It would make him bankrupt; therefore, he has rejected traditional Christianity; at this point, we do not know if he has substituted something else, but this matter will be revealed later in the play.

The central point here is the dramatic conflict between father and daughter; Shaw is presenting two opposing ways of looking at religion and life, and he is masterful in presenting the key conflict between the "maker of arms" for the armies of the world and the "savior of souls" through another type of army, and yet both armies have a motto that is similar: the "Blood and Fire" of the Salvation Army could easily apply to Undershaft's munitions factories, and Undershaft uses traditional, Christian religious imagery to describe his munitions factories, which are responsible for a "blood that cleanses" and a "fire that purifies." Cleansing and purification are the main aims of both the Salvation Army and the Undershaft and Lazarus Munitions

Foundry. Furthermore, two similar signs are used by Shaw to iden-
tify the location of the two places: the home of the Salvation Army
is at the sign of the *cross*, and the Munitions Foundry is at the sign
of the *sword*. The Cross and the Sword, then, become aligned when
the family, plus fiancés, decides to sing the militant Christian song
"Onward, Christian Soldiers," which employs the imagery of *both* the
foundry and the Christian cross.

Thus, we are brought to the basis of all drama – some type of *conflict*; now, we have the central conflict before us. Furthermore, Undershaft is seen as a tempter, another dramatic convention. In addition,
in classical dramas and in literature of all types, there is often a type
of bargain made between two people. Here, the bargain is between
Undershaft and Barbara, and at the end of the scene, it can be assumed
that Undershaft, as the temper, might be stronger than the *militant*
Major Barbara. Readers of drama should consider the type of bargain
that Faust entered into with Mephistopheles and should also consider
the number of tempters and temptations that are found in the Bible.

ACT II *(Opening Scene)*

Summary

Act II takes place in the Salvation Army Shelter, an old warehouse
which has recently been whitewashed. Two people are seen seated
in the Shelter; one is a man quite "capable of anything in reason except honesty," whose name is Snobby Price. The other is a woman
named Rummy Mitchens, who looks sixty, but is probably only forty-
five, due to the severity of her life.

As the curtain rises, Rummy asks Snobby what sort of trade he
is in. Snobby, a painter with questionable socialist leanings, uses this
opportunity to launch into an attack against the capitalistic system,
and in doing so, shows himself to be a poor specimen of mankind,
intent more on stealing, boasting, drinking, and lying that he is in
doing an honest day's work. Rummy Mitchens then confesses that
she pretends to be a worse sinner than she is because the girls at the
Salvation Army love to fuss over a real sinner. Snobby then confesses
that he is also playing the same game by making up stories about how
he abuses his "poor old mother" when, in reality, his "poor old mother"
actually beats *him* up. This playacting doesn't bother either one of

them, however, for their public confessions help bring in charitable contributions and donations; thus, they are a benefit to the Army.

Jenny Hill, a "pretty Salvation lass of eighteen," enters with Peter Shirley, a workman who is half-starved and looks half-worn out, even though he is only forty-six. He is bitter over the loss of his job to a younger man. He is very proud and will accept food only when he is assured that he can repay it later. Then suddenly, a young ruffian named Bill Walker appears in the door, blocking Jenny's exit, and he accuses her (and the Salvation Army) of turning his girlfriend against him. He is out for revenge, and he begins by roughhousing Jenny. When Rummy tries to protest, Bill Walker knocks her down with the back of his hand; then after manhandling Jenny further, he sends Jenny, Snobby, and Rummy retreating to the kitchen. Peter Shirley, however, stands up to the young bully, and he challenges him to fight someone his own age and size, instead of picking on old men and women and young girls. Shirley then taunts Bill Walker by daring him to fight against a man named Todger Fairmile, a fellow who recently joined the Salvation Army after having won a wrestling match in a public contest. Bill Walker is not so anxious to confront a professional, and so Shirley continues to taunt him. Just before Major Barbara enters, Shirley reminds Bill Walker that Barbara is the granddaughter of an Earl.

Commentary

The first part of Act II presents some of the typical inhabitants of the Salvation Army Shelter. The first two, Snobby Price and Rummy Mitchens, reveal themselves to be frauds. Shaw's point is not just to point out the hypocrisy; it is more directly aimed at suggesting that there is nothing noble or romantic about poverty. Instead of creating an atmosphere of independence, poverty breeds various types of hypocrisy, and the Salvation Army often attracts hypocrites who take advantage of the Shelters. In fact, ironically, these hypocrites contribute to the success of the Shelters because by publicly testifying their made-up confessions to sins which they never committed, they are able to enlarge the coffers of the collection plates. Shaw is also taking a sarcastic dig at a type of religion which emphasizes atonement through public confession, because once the sinner confesses and is forgiven for his sins, he is then free to sin again. In addition, Shaw disliked the theatrical aspect of public confession, which encouraged the individual to soak up the public's attention by exaggerating his own unworthiness, as is seen in the case of both Snobby Price and Rummy Mitchens.

The opening scene, furthermore, lends additional credence to Undershaft's theories later in the play – that is, by presenting us with two hypocrites who use the Salvation Army as a crutch, Undershaft's point later on that the best way to help the poor is to find them jobs and make them independent will be more convincing in the light of Snobby's and Rummy's deceit. Furthermore, when Undershaft speaks of the evils of poverty, we will already have seen this example of two people who demean themselves by confessing to lies in order to ingratiate themselves to the Army. We must constantly remember that, for Shaw, the greatest crime was poverty, and in this scene, he presents no romantic view of it; instead, he shows us the misery of the people who are gathered in an old Shelter in mid-January, shivering and hungry and lying and quarrelling.

With the arrival of Peter Shirley, we have an example of an honest poor man who has been a victim of the capitalistic class, the class which Shaw is attacking. Peter Shirley, unlike Snobby, sincerely desires to work, and he resents a system which will deny him the opportunity to work simply because he is now forty-six years old. Furthermore, it is difficult for a man who has earned his own way for his entire life to now take charity. Peter Shirley will stand, then, as a contrast to Snobby and Rummy, and he will also be a living illustration of the type of society that is needed in Undershaft's ideal socialist village, as will be revealed in the final act – a village where no one like Shirley will have to suffer the humiliation of accepting charity or will have his self-respect threatened by forces which he doesn't understand.

With the entrance of Bill Walker, Shaw introduces us to yet another type of human being, someone who will be even more instrumental to the Shelter in terms of Major Barbara's theories. He is first presented as a hardened ruffian who will tolerate no other person's opinion and who resorts to violence at a moment's notice. He will be the toughest person to convert because of his great physical power and because of his stubbornness. Through him, we will see how Barbara is the most effective person in the Salvation Army.

ACT II *(The arrival of Major Barbara at the Shelter, followed by the arrival of her father)*

Summary

After Bill Walker has been warned that Major Barbara is the granddaughter of an Earl, Bill is somewhat subdued, and then Major Barbara enters with a notebook to question the newcomers. Shirley gives his name and occupation and is assured that the Army will find him a job. Bill Walker, however, refuses to give his name, but Major Barbara recognizes him as the man whom Jenny is praying for, and she decides to put him down as "the man who – struck – poor Jenny Hill – in the mouth." Walker then demands to know the whereabouts of his girl, Mog Ebbijem, and he is told that she has gone to another Shelter and that she now has a new boyfriend named Todger Fairmile, a wrestler and a sergeant in the Salvation Army. At this point, Jenny reenters and forgives and blesses Bill Walker, causing him further consternation. At the same time, the arrival of Andrew Undershaft is announced, and Barbara ushers in her father and introduces him to Peter Shirley, who is immediately offended by Undershaft's manner of making millions, and he asserts to Undershaft: "Who made your millions for you? Me and my like. What's kep us poor? Keeping you rich. I wouldn't have your conscience, not for all your income," to which Undershaft saracastically responds: "I wouldn't have your income, not for all of your conscience, Mr. Shirley."

Undershaft then asks Barbara to continue her work as he observes her, and so she turns her attention to Bill Walker and appeals to his conscience. She is about to break through his stubborn resistance when Cusins enters beating a drum, thus breaking the spell and allowing Bill Walker to escape. Walker pities Cusins if he is to marry such a one as Barbara; he advises Cusins to "stop er jawr," or else Cusins will suffer for it. At this point, Barbara has to leave, and she tells Cusins to explain to her father how the Shelter functions.

Commentary

This scene shows Major Barbara going about her business of soothing and converting souls to the Salvation Army. She is indeed the epitome of the efficient businesswoman as she busies herself with taking notes on Peter Shirley, his job situation, and then promising him that she will find work for him. She is the essence of tact when Shirley loudly proclaims that he is a Secularist (that is, one who believes that the well-being of mankind takes precedence over religious observations); Major Barbara very calmly tells him that her father is also a Secularist. She then shows herself to be highly accomplished in dealing with difficult or antagonistic characters such as Bill Walker. Of course, we should be aware that Bill Walker has already been somewhat intimidated by the knowledge that Major Barbara is the granddaughter of an Earl. Even though Shaw – the man – deplored such class distinctions, Shaw – the dramatist – was well aware of the common man's awe of nobility, and he used this fact for dramatic purposes. However, Major Barbara, on her own, proves to be quite capable of handling the situation. She is aware that Walker has struck old Rummy Mitchens and that he has treated Jenny Hill in a brutal fashion. Major Barbara, however, does not reprimand him. Instead, when Walker refuses to give his name, she records him in her book as "the man who – struck – poor little Jenny Hill – in the mouth." Instead of reproaching him, Major Barbara lets him know that Jenny is praying for him. Had someone scolded him or cursed him, it would have had no effect, but this unexpected behavior causes his conscience to twinge slightly, and Major Barbara is aware of the effect that she is achieving, and she skillfully exploits this aspect of Bill's character.

In the next interchange, where Bill Walker volunteers to atone (the fact that he even considers atonement attests to Major Barbara's effectiveness) for hitting Jenny Hill by having himself beat up by Todger Fairmile, Major Barbara rejects this approach; she will not allow Bill Walker to buy salvation from the Salvation Army by having someone blacken his eyes because he did the same thing to Jenny Hill. As Major Barbara says: "two black eyes won't make one white one." She believes, like Shaw, that a man must change inwardly. Too much forgiveness simply allows the sinner to return to his sinning with the knowledge that he can be forgiven again. Consequently, Major Barbara is trying to get Bill Walker to redeem himself through a change in his conscience – not through someone else's forgiveness.

Thus, Major Barbara is seen as the completely self-assured, confident person who is able to control the various "minor" types at the Shelter. With the arrival of Barbara's father, the question will be whether or not she will be able to control him.

ACT II [Scene between Undershaft and Cusins]

Summary

Undershaft immediately suspects the sincerity of Cusins's attachment, as well as his involvement with the Salvation Army, and with a flourish of the drum sticks, Cusins lets Undershaft know that he is right in his assumptions, but Cusins points out that he is a "collector of religions," and he has found that he can believe them all. Undershaft then explains his own personal religion, which is based on money and gunpowder; the traditional values ("honor, justice, truth, love, mercy, and so forth") are only "graces and luxuries of a rich, strong, and safe life." Forced to choose between traditional values and "money and gunpowder," Undershaft would always choose the latter because until one has the power brought about by money, one cannot afford the luxury of the other "graces."

While not disagreeing, Cusins points out that Undershaft will have to choose between Barbara and his, Undershaft's, own unique religion—and, he states, Barbara won't tolerate Undershaft's views. Undershaft agrees but he also points out that Cusins faces the same problem because Barbara will soon find out that Cusins's drum, which he plays for the Army, is "hollow." Now it is Cusins's turn to be open and honest, and he maintains that he enjoys the Army because it is an army of "joy, of love, of courage. . . . it marches to fight the devil with trumpet and drum, with music and dancing, [and that] it takes [a] poor professor of Greek" and gives him shelter and a drum so he can beat Greek dithyrambs throughout the streets. He is rhapsodic about the Army, but as Undershaft knows, not for reasons that Barbara would understand. Thus, Cusins's frankness wins Undershaft's confidence, and they both enter into a bargain to win Barbara over to their sides:

> UNDERSHAFT: Professor Cusins: you are a young man after my own heart.
>
> CUSINS: Mr. Undershaft: you are, as far as I am able to gather, a most infernal old rascal, but you appeal very strongly to my sense of ironic humor.

Undershaft, who has become extremely attached to his daughter Barbara and recognizes in her something unusual, something beyond the call of the ordinary person, maintains that they must convert her to his point of view, which is money and gunpowder, which will, in turn, offer "freedom and power." He convinces Cusins by asking him if anyone except a madman can make cannons as he does, and can anyone except a madman translate Euripides as Cusins does, and can anyone who is really sane convert poor people? Thus, there are three "mad" people (Undershaft, Cusins, and Barbara) in the Shelter today, and they must all work together in order to raise the common person up to their level of existence. Cusins then points out that Barbara is in love with the common man, but Undershaft rises to his most magnificent heights when he points out the absurdity of Barbara's love of the poor and her attachment to poverty: after all, he says, even the saints who professed love for such things were absurd. No one can *really* love disease, suffering, dirt, and poverty. Love for such things would be unnatural, a perversion of all values. For Undershaft, a love of poverty has no romance in it because he himself endured poverty as a child, and there is nothing noble or romantic about being poor. He concludes: "We three must stand together above the common people: how else can we help their children to climb up beside us? Barbara must belong to us, not to the Salvation Army." When Cusins points out that Barbara cannot be bought, Undershaft agrees, but he then points out that the Salvation Army *can* be bought — precisely because all "religious organizations exist by selling themselves to the rich." Once he can buy the Army and then have Barbara, he will prove to her that rather than her working for the poor, it would be better if she were to work for the sober, honest, happy worker, he who is not in physical want of food and nourishment.

Commentary

This scene sets forth some of Shaw's paradoxes: for example, the one thing that Undershaft, his daughter, and Cusins have in common is a type of madness — that is, only a madman would make cannons and other instruments of destruction as Undershaft does; only a madman would attempt to translate the wild Euripides from ancient Greek to modern English as Cusins does, and only a madwoman would attempt to covert such hypocritical sinners as Barbara does. Thus, the paradox is that these three mad people must combine and work together to raise the common person "up" to their level. This will be ironically accomplished by buying them — by "owning" them.

Undershaft's main point and Shaw's ultimate point is that *poverty* is the worst of all crimes. Having lived in poverty himself, Undershaft finds no romance in dirt, and there is no need for him to pretend that poverty is a blessing; for him, poverty has never made anyone better off: ". . . leave it to the coward to make a religion of his cowardice by preaching humility." Generally, Undershaft and Shaw believe that anyone who supports a system of government that tolerates poverty has to share in the responsibility for the poverty. In Undershaft's (and Shaw's) ideal state, poverty will be totally eliminated, and everyone will work according to their capacities.

ACT II *(The return of Major Barbara, accompanied by Shirley, Snobby Price, and Jenny Hill)*

Summary

Major Barbara returns with Shirley, Snobby, and Jenny in an exhilarated mood; the meeting has been a great success. After they count the money, however, they are two pence short of their goal of five shillings. Barbara feels that much of the success of the meeting was due to Snobby Price's narration of how he used to beat up his mother before he was reformed: Barbara even says that "if you had given your poor mother just one more kick, we should have got the whole five shillings!" Barbara's father then offers to give the two pence so as to round out the amount, but after Barbara inquires about the manner by which his two pence were earned, and Undershaft responds that he earned the pence by selling cannons, torpedoes, submarines, etc., Barbara refuses the money and says that he will have to work out his own salvation – he can't *buy* it with his ill-earned pence. When he offers still more money, Barbara adamantly refuses that offer also, maintaining that "two million millions would not be enough. There is bad blood on your hands; and nothing but good blood can cleanse them."

At the same time, however, Major Barbara bemoans the fact that she must spend so much of her time collecting money, for she does not have enough time, she feels, to strive for people's souls. Her ideal aim is to convert people, not to always be "begging for the Army in a way I'd die sooner than beg for myself." But she also recognizes that she can't talk religion to a man with bodily hunger. Major Barbara, however, is confident that money will come because a Mrs. Baines, a high-ranking member of the Army, prayed for money last night, and her prayers are *always* answered, and, furthermore, Major Barbara announces that Mrs. Baines wants to meet Mr. Undershaft.

At this point, Bill Walker enters and tells how he had his encounter with Todger Fairmile, who refused to fight with him (even when Bill Walker spit on him); instead, Todger pinned Walker to the ground, and he and Mog prayed for Bill's hard heart to be softened. Now he wants to give some money to Jenny Hill to make up for having treated her so brutally, but Major Barbara refuses to accept the money; once again she asserts that "the Army is not to be bought." She says, "We want your soul, Bill; and we'll take nothing less." Undershaft then offers another of his temptations: if Major Barbara will accept Bill Walker's one pound note, he will match it with the other ninety-nine pounds to make the sum a round one hundred pounds. Again, Major Barbara refuses: the Salvation Army is not to be bought! – even for "thirty pieces of silver," the traditional going price to pay for anyone who is for sale. Bill Walker then throws his sovereign on the drum, saying, "Take it or leave it."

Commentary

This scene is filled with ironies and paradoxes, most of which are unknown to Major Barbara. Yet surely the audience would find it comic when Barbara maintains that if Snobby Price had given his mother just *one more kick* and then narrated the entire sequence of events to the crowd, the Army would have gotten even more money. Again, since we, the audience, know that Snobby is only pretending so as to please the crowd, the hypocrisy is apparent to everyone *except* Major Barbara. Thus, for the audience, the integrity of the Salvation Army's willingness to take money from such sources as Snobby's false, hypocritical confessions leads us to the idea of whether or not the Army can take a contribution from a munitions manufacturer. Where does hypocrisy lie – if one is willing to accept one man's contributions (Snobby's hypocritical contributions) and refusing others (Bill Walker's sovereign and Undershaft's offer of, first, two pence, and then later, his offer of ninety-nine pounds)?

Major Barbara's assertion to her father that "you can't buy your salvation here for two pence" becomes doubly ironic in the next scene when he is able to buy it for five thousand pounds, thus showing us that *any* organization has a price that it can be bought for. At the same time, Shaw presents a paradox concerning the need for keeping the Shelter open during the winter. If the Shelter is closed, then many starving people will be without food or shelter and "the starvation this winter is beating us; everybody is unemployed." Consequently, the problem that faces any such organization is this: can such an organization do its charitable work if the only way that it can do so is to accept "tainted" money? If the Army does not accept Undershaft's money, then the Shelter will have to close down and can serve no function; furthermore, this will then allow untold numbers of people to suffer and perhaps die. While Major Barbara bemoans the fact that she has to think more of collecting money than collecting souls, and that she "can't talk religion to a man with bodily hunger in his eyes," we are then prepared for the last act of the play, where Barbara will be presented to the citizens of Perivale St. Andrews, who are well fed and happy; to these people, she can then present her religious views without worrying about her audience's bodily needs.

Another irony is the introduction of Mrs. Baines, the commissioner for the Army, who prayed for money, then arranged for a meeting with such wealthy people as Bodger, the brewer, and with the munitions maker, Undershaft. We must remember that her prayers for money have always been answered, and if she is to meet with Undershaft, we can predict that her prayers will again be answered—to the tune of a large check from Undershaft.

At the end of this scene, Bill Walker returns to describe his encounter with Todger Fairmile. Again the bully whom we dislike is now seen as a man truly troubled in his conscience, and he doesn't know how to soothe it. He offers to pay Jenny Hill for the physical damage he has done, and when this is rejected, he tries to make a contribution to the Army to salve his conscience. Again, Major Barbara refuses to let him buy forgiveness with a small financial contribution. As noted above, Major Barbara firmly believes, as does Shaw, that one cannot buy forgiveness because that would allow one to go out and sin again. Instead, there must be an inward change of attitude: Major Barbara says, "We want your soul, Bill; and we'll take nothing less." Again, her father is seen as the tempter, as he suggests that if she accepts Bill's one pound note, then he will round it out to one hundred pounds by giving the other ninety-nine pounds. Using the appropriate religious imagery, she tells Undershaft that they cannot be bought for thirty pieces of silver (alluding, of course, to the thirty pieces of silver that Judas received for betraying Christ). But while Major Barbara is in the *business* of converting souls and in the business of collecting money, she is making so many arbitrary decisions about the source of the money that she is offered, that she is now standing on dangerous grounds. First, the temptation was only for two pence – which she refused; then Undershaft upped the price to ninety-nine pounds, which Barbara also refused; the next temptation will be so high that even though Barbara will refuse it, the Salvation Army cannot afford to refuse it.

Finally, the question is this: at what price is salvation to be bought? Bill Walker raises this question. Even though the Army does not accept his small contribution, which he lays on the drum, he is becoming aware of the possible double standard involved – that is, while refusing his small contribution, the Army will accept the larger donation to be made by Undershaft, a fact that will make Bill utter, "Wot prawce selvytion nah?" (i.e., "What price salvation now?").

ACT II *(The Appearance of Mrs. Baines)*

Summary

At this moment, Mrs. Baines, a Salvation Army Commissioner, arrives and meets Undershaft. She enthusiastically describes the work of the Salvation Army (even to the point of keeping the poor fed enough so that they won't strike against the capitalists), and she ecstatically tells of the offer made by a man named Bodger, England's chief manufacturer of gin, beef, and whiskey. Bodger will give the Army five thousand pounds if a donor, or donors, can be found to match this contribution. Undershaft gladly writes a check for this sum, to the utter horror of Barbara and to the cynical amazement of Bill Walker, who asks her again: "What price salvation now?"

Barbara immediately tries to get Mrs. Baines to reconsider, because so many of the people whom they attend to are people who have become drunkards because of Bodger's whiskey and gin. Mrs. Baines, however, answers that "Lord Saxmundham has a soul to be saved like any of us. If heaven has found the way to make a good use of his money, are we to set ourselves up against the answer to our prayers?" Both Undershaft and Mrs. Baines argue with Barbara –

Undershaft pointing out that simply because less than one per cent of the poor misuse alcohol is no reason to blame the man who makes it; then Mrs. Baines wonders if "there will be less drinking or more if all those poor souls we are saving come tomorrow and find the doors of our Shelters shut in their faces." In fact, Lord Saxmundham is giving money to take away from his own business. Undershaft continues the argument because his contribution is to be used to bring peace on earth, and every time a war is halted, he will lose large amounts of money: "I am never richer, never busier than when the papers are full of war. Well, it is your work to preach peace on earth and good will to men. . . . Every convert you make is a vote against war . . . yet I give you this money to help you to hasten my own commercial ruin." He then presents the check, which is accepted with flourishes of drum sticks and tears of joy from all gathered round.

In the celebration that follows, Cusins is delighted with the paradoxical irony of the entire proceedings and calls for a great meeting at once so that Major Barbara can announce that the Army is saved – and saved because of Mr. Andrew Undershaft. Cusins then gets a flag and a trombone for Undershaft, instructing him to "Blow, Machiavelli, blow" as they are about to leave the Shelter triumphantly.

Suddenly, Major Barbara announces that she can't come. She does not criticize Mrs. Baines, but instead, she takes her "Silver S brooch" from her collar and pins the badge on her father's lapel. They leave together to the cry of "Blood and Fire," with Undershaft crying, "My ducats and my daughter!" Cusins then cries out, "Money and gunpowder!" (the Undershaft and Lazarus motto), and Barbara, in a cry of despair asks, "Drunkenness and Murder! My God: why has thou forsaken me?"

After they all have left, Bill Walker wants to retrieve his money, which was earlier not acceptable to the Salvation Army (according to Barbara), but to his dismay, he finds that it is gone and he hears that the "pious" Snobby Price, after having made his public confessions, at "half past twelve . . . pinched [Bill Walker's] pound at a quarter to two." When Barbara promises to refund him his pound, Bill Walker will not be bought by her, and so he leaves again, taunting her with "What price salvation now?" Barbara examines her funds and talks Peter Shirley into accompanying her for a cup of tea to keep her from crying.

Commentary

Everything has been leading up to this dramatic scene. As noted in the last scene, Major Barbara adheres to her principles. In the same manner that she would not let Bill Walker pay for his conscience, and in the manner that she would not accept the two pence and then later, she would not accept the ninety-nine pounds from her father because, according to her, the money was "tainted," likewise she is not willing to accept the five thousand pounds because, regardless of the sum, it comes from the same source. However, because of the huge amount of money to be collected, Major Barbara is defeated by outside forces; she cannot withstand the arguments of Mrs. Baines and the other Salvationists who look upon the donations of Bodger and Undershaft as the salvation of the Salvation Army. The central paradox is presented by Mrs. Baines (even though she is not intellectually aware of the paradox): can "tainted money" be accepted to be used for the execution of worthwhile ends?

Part of the dramatic irony (which means that we, the audience, know things that one or more characters on the stage do not know) is that Mrs. Baines thinks that she has been successful in soliciting the five thousand pounds from Undershaft, but we, the readers and the audience, know from the preceding scene that Undershaft has announced his intentions of *buying* the Salvation Army. He first accomplishes this intellectually by pointing out that in a perfect society, he and Bodger would cease to exist—that is, in the ideal society that Major Barbara is working to achieve, there would be no need for the average person to resort to alcohol or to become an alcoholic; thus, Bodger, the distiller, is working against his own self-interests in giving money to an organization which advocates complete abstinence. Likewise, in the perfect society, there would be no need for munitions of any sort; thus, Undershaft's donation would destroy him *if* the Salvation Army is right and is persuasive in advocating peace on earth. But Undershaft's ultimate aim is to undermine Barbara's belief in the Salvation Army and thus to free her from its claims so that she can join him in his great socialistic design.

Mrs. Baines's argument for the poor must not be misinterpreted. She pleads for money so that the poor won't attack the rich. That is, if the poor are given just a small amount—enough to subsist on— then the capitalists will be free to continue their exploitation of the poor. Shaw would be totally opposed to this type of exploitation and

and would advocate the poor's revolting against the capitalistic class. Shaw, like others, is opposed to the Salvation Army's using food, confessions, or any type of "opiate" to salve the conscience of the masses into passively accepting the dictum that a poverty class is necessary in a capitalistic society. The reader should constantly be aware that, for Shaw, poverty was the worst of all crimes (the use of the term "crime" to apply to poverty is a highly controversial use of the word), and that all types of charity contribute to the acceptance of poverty as the natural state of existence.

Cusins, who says little in this scene, but nevertheless supports Undershaft, constantly refers to Undershaft as a "Machiavelli"—that is, as a person who will use any means to get his way. Undershaft wants to win Barbara over to his side for the most altruistic reasons, and therefore he will use any unscrupulous means to accomplish this end, which is theoretically an end aimed at the betterment of the general state of mankind.

The final statements that ring so true are Bill Walker's statements "What price salvation now" and "I ain't to be bought," because the salvation of Bodger and Undershaft costs them five thousand pounds each and Bill Walker offered only one pound, which had been both rejected and stolen from him, and whereas he had tried earlier to *buy* his salvation, he now throws the concept back at Major Barbara with his assertion that "I ain't to be bought" because now the Salvation Army itself has been bought.

Barbara's removing her Salvation Army pin and crying, "My God: why hast thou forsaken me?" indicates that she has been defeated. How she will accept her defeat will be the subject of the next act.

ACT III *(Lady Britomart's Library)*

Summary

This act opens the next morning in Lady Britomart's library, and we are immediately astonished to see Major Barbara dressed *not* in her Salvation Army uniform, but in an "ordinary fashionable dress." Charles Lomax, trying to console Barbara, makes an inopportune remark about there being "a certain amount of tosh about the Salvation Army." Adolphus enters in a questionable state of sobriety and announces that he has "been making a night of it" with Andrew Undershaft, whom he calls "the Prince of Darkness" and who, he says, has plied Adolphus with plentiful amounts of Spanish burgundy, even though Undershaft himself is a teetotaler.

Barbara inquires about the Salvation Army meeting and learns that it was a tremendous success with a hundred and seventeen conversions, in addition to many prayers said for Bodger, as well as prayers for the anonymous donor of five thousand pounds to the Army. At this moment, Morrison, the butler, announces the arrival of Andrew Undershaft, and Lady Britomart sends everyone out so that she can confront Andrew alone about the family's affairs.

Andrew Undershaft genially concedes to Lady Britomart's stipulation about Barbara's and Sarah's need for money. But when Lady Britomart broaches the subject of their son, Stephen, Undershaft loses all interest, maintaining that Stephen doesn't show the slightest resemblance to either of them; moreover, he asserts that Stephen *might* be able to learn the rudimentary mechanics of running the office routines of the munitions foundry, but that he certainly has no aptitude for managing the entire Undershaft and Lazarus empire. Furthermore, Undershaft is determined to remain true to the Undershaft tradition of leaving the foundry to a foundling – a "tradition" that has never been broken. He admits, however, that he has not yet found a suitable successor; everyone whom he has found is "exactly like Stephen" – inept. Undershaft is searching for a man who has not yet been corrupted by conventional ideas – a man whose outstanding qualities are a strong will and an independent turn of mind. He tells Lady Britomart to find such a foundling, and he will be willing to marry him off to Barbara, thus keeping "the foundry in the family."

Stephen enters then, and after some sharp conversational exchanges, he makes it quite clear – to both his father and his mother – that he has absolutely no interest and absolutely no capacity for managing such a business as the munitions foundry: "I repudiate the cannon business."

Undershaft is so relieved that he promises to help Stephen get established in another career; after all, Undershaft says, "I owe you a fair start in life in exchange for disinheriting you." After further discussion concerning Stephen's aptitudes, Stephen confesses that his supreme quality is that he knows "the difference between right and wrong." This statement utterly fascinates Undershaft since this is the single philosophical distinction that has baffled all of the wisest philosophers and intellects throughout the ages. He scoffs at his son, but Stephen manages to keep his temper, even if with difficulty.

Yet Stephen objects to a derogatory statement which his father makes about politics, for Undershaft begins lecturing his son upon the reality of who it is who *really* runs the country; the real rulers, Undershaft says, are the people who have power and use it to control the masses. Stephen responds – as best he can – with a few well-chosen cliches about the importance of national character as being the true power responsible for the operation of the government, and Undershaft announces that Stephen has just discovered his career: Stephen will be a journalist, and, in this way, Stephen can profit from his high-sounding moral cliches.

Before Stephen has a chance to retaliate to this suggestion, the others return, ready for their journey to the Lazarus and Undershaft Munitions Foundry. Barbara and Cusins will go with Undershaft in a new bulletproof vehicle which he is experimenting with; the others will follow in the carriage. Before they leave, Barbara is convinced that she is about to experience some infernal "pit where lost creatures with blackened faces stir up smoky fires and are driven and tormented by my father." Undershaft explains that it is quite the contrary: "It is a spotless clean and beautiful hillside town," where it is not necessary that he ever give any orders because of the natural propensity of the Englishman to keep people below them in tow and to have such awe for rank and privilege that he never feels a need to be dictatorial.

When Barbara then tells him that although she will keep her bargain and visit his "factory of death," she will never forgive him for destroying the soul of a man (Bill Walker) whom she was on the verge of saving only the day before; to kill physically with cannons, Barbara says, is one thing, but to kill another man's soul is unforgivable. When Undershaft very cleverly reminds her that one cannot "strike a man to the heart and leave no mark on him," Barbara then joyfully realizes that her father is right – even though Cusins sees it as the cunning of "the Prince of Darkness."

Commentary

This first scene presents the results of last night's breakup. While the scene is partly light social comedy, yet all of the serious themes of the play are reinforced. With the entrance of Cusins, we learn, for example, that last night's rally was a tremendous success and that Cusins spent the evening drinking wine with Undershaft, who is a teetotaler. Essentially, Shaw's men of purpose (such as Undershaft) are often more concerned with destiny and their own force on life than with wasting their time drinking. Thus, Undershaft's purpose last night was apparently to influence Cusins and to discover how Cusins could be "used" by Undershaft. But Cusins does not admit that it was Undershaft who made him drunk; instead, he insists that it was Dionysus who possessed him. Instead of Cusins's gaining salvation through the Salvation Army, we now see that Cusins is going to achieve salvation through an *emotional*, Dionysian wisdom; that is, through a rejection of moral conformity. The contrast is comic: into the very proper drawing room comes an intellectual drunk, rejecting propriety and social decorum in favor of some sort of wild Dionysian power.

In the brief scene between Lady Britomart and Undershaft, we have the final turn of the plot introduced. Undershaft has admitted that he cannot find a foundling to take over the foundry, and he asks Lady Britomart to find one, and then they can marry off the foundling to Barbara and thus keep the foundry in the family. This prepares the plot for the unique way that Cusins – as a foundling – will be able to both marry Barbara and keep the foundry in the family.

The scene between Stephen and his father is high comedy. In spite of Lady Britomart's protestations that breeding is more important than anything (thus Stephen, who is well-bred, should inherit the foundry), yet everything that Stephen says or does shows him to be completely inept and incapable of doing anything except uttering high-sounding cliches. When he maintains that he, at least, knows the difference between "right and wrong," he is not even intelligent enough to know that since the very beginning of philosophy, that very subject has been among the main concerns of mankind's greatest minds. For Stephen to be so flippant is comic; for Stephen not to even know how absurd he is is incredulous. Thus, Andrew Undershaft is only more confirmed than ever in his decision to be faithful to the Undershaft tradition and find a man of unusual potential; Stephen is clearly fit only to spout high-toned cliches.

Shaw also uses this scene for another of his attacks on politics. One should remember this point when Undershaft tells Stephen that if he can't do anything else, then he should go into politics; Shaw was keenly aware that there would probably be many members of Parliament in the audience. In addition, Shaw is being brutally realistic when he points out that it is power and money which influence government – not individuals and character.

We should remember that this is the turning point for Barbara. As the great tempters of the past have come from infernal pits of hellfire and damnation, Barbara (whose soul will now be tempted) envisions the Undershaft foundry in images of smoky fires. The image, of course, is also the image of the ugly nineteenth century factory – a very real place of death and destruction. Barbara's soul, then, will be won when she sees that the town, as described by her father, really does exist – that the "death and destruction" factory has created an ideal social community where everyone is happy and contented with their lives.

ACT III *(A hill or platform overlooking the town of Perivale St. Andrews.)*

Summary

The setting of this scene is a platform on a hill overlooking the model village of Perivale St. Andrews, and the area is surrounded with "several dummy soldiers more or less mutilated." Major Barbara – now merely 'Barbara,' as in the preceding scene – is seen alone, observing the entire valley. Cusins enters, admiring the perfection of the place, and he informs Barbara that they have indeed found employment for Peter Shirley, but that the man is frightfully unhappy because the job involves "mental time-keeping," and that Shirley is uncomfortable in the refined lodgings that they have provided for him.

Next, Stephen arrives, filled with enthusiasm for the place. Cusins agrees with him and says that everything is "horribly, frightfully, immorally, unanswerably perfect." Then Sarah arrives, exclaiming about the magnificent facilities that are available. Then Andrew Undershaft enters with the good news that the new Lazarus and Undershaft battleship is a huge success: "It wiped out a fort with three hundred soldiers in it" in the Manchurian War, but, as yet, he doesn't know which side mastered this victory. Stephen compliments his father on the "wonderful forethought, the power of organizatioin, the administrative capacity, the financial genius, the colossal capital" that the community represents, but he wonders if things aren't *too* perfect. Undershaft responds by pointing out that there *is* a certain built-in anxiety because "we may be blown to smithereens at any moment."

Bilton, the foreman, arrives with Charles Lomax from inside the high explosives shelter where Lomax had carelessly lit a cigarette and dropped the lighted match on the floor. Lomax ignores the seriousness of his actions and thinks that the precautions are "a bit of tosh."

Lady Britomart arrives then, and as fits her concerns, she is terribly impressed with all the domestic arrangements, but she is unhappy at the thought that all of this magnificence might pass into someone else's hands. She even goes so far as to suggest that Cusins be made the successor, and Undershaft is quite willing because Cusins is the exact type whom he is looking for, but, unfortunately, Cusins is *not* a foundling. By a clever ruse, then, Cusins points out that this objection *could* be overcome because, *technically*, while his parents' marriage is legal in Australia—in England, "My mother is my father's deceased wife's sister and in this island I am consequently a foundling." By this subterfuge, Undershaft acknowledges that Cusins is *indeed* eligible to be an heir. However, Cusins is not so easily persuaded to take the job: he says, "There is an abyss of moral horror between me and your accursed aerial battleships."

In spite of all the differences, however, it is agreed that Cusins will take over if a proper bargain can be struck, with Cusins demanding much more money and a share of the profits, and Undershaft reluctantly agreeing—if Cusins agrees to the basic code of the Armorer—that is, Cusins must sell weapons to all people, regardless of the principles of the men who are buying the weapons, and, furthermore, that Cusins is willing to change his name (Adolphus Cusins) to Andrew Undershaft.

Cusins has no difficulty deciding whether or not to change his name, but he does have difficulty with the moral question. Undershaft maintains, however, that one can make weapons, but one cannot make men of courage and conviction. He then turns to Barbara and addresses her: it is easy, he says, to convert men's souls by promising them bread and treacle to eat. Poverty will force men to agree to *anything*. In fact, poverty is the worst of all crimes. He then challenges her to scrap her old ideas in the same way that he would scrap a bad plan or a bad idea. Come to this model town, he says, where everything is cleanliness and prosperity and test her theories.

Undershaft further maintains that since poverty is the most heinous of crimes, destroying more men and affecting society in a worse way than do wars or pestilence, more than murders and robbers, then it must be done away with. When Barbara is reluctant to leave her wards in London's East End, Undershaft reminds her that he himself was once a member of the poverty stricken East End, and he can assure her that there is nothing good about poverty; let her bring her Bill Walker with her, and she can save him from poverty – then, when he is comfortable physically, Barbara can more firmly meet the challenge of saving his soul.

When Undershaft turns to Cusins for a decision, Cusins maintains that he wants to "avoid being a rascal." Undershaft rejects such appeals to love, pity, and personal righteousness as being of no social value; if you want to change society, he says in effect, you have to have a large amount of money to do so. When Cusins ultimately maintains that he "hates war," then Undershaft challenges him to take a position so as to become powerful enough to "make war on war" – in other words, take the position as chief of the munitions factory.

Undershaft leaves then to show the others the inside of one of the munitions shelters.

Left alone, Cusins tells Barbara that he is going to accept the offer. When Barbara mentions Cusins's having "sold his soul," Cusins tells her that he has sold his soul for lesser things – for taxes, for professorships, for income, and so forth, and now he will sell it "for reality and power" – not for himself, but for the world. He emphasizes that cannons do not kill people by exploding themselves; people must set them off, and he now realizes that one "cannot have power for good without having power for evil too." He wants to use power to bring about a sense of equality among men – that is, he wants to give the common person a weapon to use against tyranny of any type.

Suddenly, Barbara agrees with him that he has made the right decision. She also realizes that her work with the Salvation Army was misdirected: "Turning our backs on Bodger and Undershaft is turning our backs on life." She further realizes that the wicked and evil in the world are also a part of the totality of life. She now sees that trying to save men's souls by giving them "a scrap of bread and treacle" in return for which there has been their "sobbing with gratitude" is no longer an acceptable approach. She maintains: "My father shall never throw it in my teeth again that my converts were bribed with bread." Now she will convert only well-fed men and women, and with her faith once again restored, Major Barbara returns to the colors!

Commentary

This scene is set, paradoxically, at a place where the peaceful valley of Perivale St. Andrews is viewed from a perspective where it is surrounded by the symbols of death and destruction. The lovely perfection of the model town is seen against an immediate foreground of cannons and dummy, straw soldiers which have been theoretially destroyed by the instruments of destruction created by Andrew Undershaft. Furthermore, all of the characters are standing next to one of the explosive shafts, and they can thus be blown up at any minute. Consequently, the physical surroundings comment upon the philosophical discussion – the contrast is as great as between Lady Britomart's insistence upon formalized rituals and Undershaft's insistence upon the right of many to destroy all types of rituals and to establish new governments and new religions. Thus, all of the discussions concerning peace, brotherhood, religion, and social security take place, paradoxically, amidst the instruments of destruction and the fake bodies of mutilated soldiers; furthermore, everyone is standing upon a hill which could at any moment explode and shatter each of them in infinitesimal pieces.

At the beginning of the scene, Shaw dramatically has each of the characters enter and admire various aspects of the model city. Since each character had expected to see some fiery pit of hell, a pit of horrible filth and stench filled with degenerate and filthy people, they are constantly surprised by the perfection of this place. This is Shaw's statement concerning the socialistic state. That is, only the rich can afford to establish the perfect socialistic state which in St. Perivale is also seen as the ideal utopian settlement, as attested to by the various reactions of each character. Stephen is impressed with the schools and the libraries, and he acknowledges that the entire place is a "perfect triumph of modern industry." He acknowledges to his father that the place represents "wonderful forethought, power of organization, administrative capacity [and] financial genius." Lady Britomart is overwhelmed by all of the domestic arrangements, and Barbara and Cusins are awed by the entire concept.

Ultimately, this final scene serves as the vehicle for Shaw's main ideas. First, Shaw (through Undershaft) reemphasizes the idea that poverty is the worst of all evils. Undershaft was brought up in London's East End amidst the worst types of poverty, and he assures his listeners that there is nothing romantic, charming, or attractive about poverty. Instead, he says, poverty is the most destructive thing known to man, rendering man a victim of filth, disease, and crime. Thus, Undershaft is the ultimate realist, and yet he is also a quasi-mystic. He strongly feels that bodies are to be saved first and then their spiritual needs can be tended to. This is the challenge which he confronts Major Barbara with; he challenges her to bring the Bill Walkers of the world to St. Perivale and give them physical security (freedom from want and hunger), and then, once the masses feel materially secure, Major Barbara can work to save their souls.

To change the world, Undershaft maintains that a person of great wealth, power, and imagination is needed. Cusins could be that person. As for Cusins, he is strongly attracted to Undershaft's argument to use his power to "make war on war." Thus, ultimately, Cusins will accept Undershaft's challenge, and Major Barbara will also acknowledge the value of saving the body first and then wrestling with the soul.

SUGGESTED THEME TOPICS

1. Discuss the relationship between Shaw's Preface and with the drama as a whole.

2. Discuss the various paradoxes and ironies that run throughout the drama.

3. Discuss the differences between Undershaft's and Major Barbara's commitments to the improvement of mankind.

4. Discuss Undershaft and Cusins as Shaw's ideal "superman."

5. In spite of its intellectual basis, *Major Barbara* is considered to be one of Shaw's major comedies. Discuss the various comic techniques that Shaw uses to keep his audience involved in the action of the play.

SAINT JOAN NOTES

GENERAL PLOT SUMMARY

In 1429 A.D., a young country girl known simply as Joan of Arc, or sometimes simply as The Maid, is given an interview by Robert de Baudricourt since she will not leave until she speaks with him. She tells him that she needs horses and armor to go to the Dauphin of France and to raise the seige of Orleans, a city held captive by the English forces. She knows that a seige would be possible because the voices of Saints Margaret and Catherine have told her what to do. Upon being convinced by The Maid's simplicity, Captain de Baudricourt grants her request.

Upon arriving at the Dauphin's castle, The Maid encounters all sorts of difficulties, especially with the Dauphin who wants nothing to do with wars and fighting. When France's military fortunes and predicament are reviewed, Joan's demands that something be done to improve France's condition fall on deaf ears, but when she is alone with the Dauphin, she is able to instill enough courage in him so that he finally consents to let her lead the army, knowing full well that she can't make France's condition worse.

Joan then goes to the Loire River near Orleans, where she encounters Dunois, the commander of the French forces; he explains the necessity of waiting until the wind changes, but Joan is determined to lead her forces against the English stronghold without waiting; suddenly, the wind does change favorably, and Dunois pledges his allegiance to The Maid.

Some time later, in the English camp, Warwick, the leader of the English forces, and his chaplain, de Stogumber, are maintaining that The Maid must be a witch because there is no other way of accounting for the heavy English losses and defeats except by sorcery.

The Bishop of Beauvais, Peter Cauchon, enters and discusses the fate of Joan of Arc. Cauchon's principal intellectual concern is that Joan is setting up her own private conscience in place of the authority of the Church. Warwick, who is not influenced by the concerns of the Church, is, instead, concerned that Joan is telling the common people and the serfs to pledge their allegiance directly to the king, whereas the entire feudal system is based upon the lower classes pledging their allegiance to their immediate lords and masters. Joan's simple pleas can possibly destroy the entire feudal system. Cauchon also adds that Joan is trying to get the common people to pledge further allegiance to their native countries (France and England), instead of to the Universal Catholic Church, an act which would further lessen the power of the Church. Thus, for different reasons, both agree that The Maid must be put to death.

After more victories, Joan has finally been able to fulfill her promise to drive the English back and have the Dauphin crowned king in the Cathedral at Rheims. After the ceremony, Joan is anxious to move on and capture Paris and drive the English from the city. The Dauphin, however, is content now with what he has recaptured, Commander Dunois is hesitant to start another campaign after all of the recent successes, and the Archbishop is beginning to find Joan to be too proud and defiant. Joan then realizes that she must stand *alone* in the same way that "saints have always stood alone," and in spite of the warning that if she falls into the enemy's hands, neither the military, nor the state, nor the Church will lift a hand to rescue her.

Some nine months later, Joan is standing trial for heresy. She has been imprisoned and in chains for these nine months and has been questioned many times about the validity of her "voices." After many complicated theological questions, her accusers force Joan to admit that her voices were not heavenly sent voices, but, instead, came from Satan. After her recantation of the voices, her judges then sentence her to perpetual imprisonment and isolation, living off only bread and water. Joan rejects this horrid punishment and tears up her recantation. She is immediately carried to the stake and burnt as a witch; afterward, the Executioner enters and announces that Joan's heart would not burn.

Some twenty-five years later, in an Epilogue, Joan reappears before the King (the former Dauphin) and her chief accusers, who have now been condemned by a subsequent court, which has pronounced Joan innocent of all charges and her judges guilty of all sorts of crimes.

The time then moves to 1920, when Joan is declared to be a saint by the Church. As such, she now has the power to return as a living woman, and she asks everyone present if she *should* return. This is a horrifying prospect for them all, and they all confess that they wish her to remain dead. Joan then asks of God, "O Lord, how long before the world will be ready to accept its saints?"

LIST OF CHARACTERS

Joan of Arc, often referred to, simply, as The Maid

Joan is, of course, the central character of the play. Based upon the historical character, Shaw presents her as a simple country girl who is uneducated but not unintelligent. For the public, Joan, according to Shaw's Preface, offers her brilliant ideas in terms of voices from heaven which speak to her. Early in the play, she establishes her superiority in terms of military tactics and strategy, always knowing where to place the cannons and other artillery. Until her capture, she proves that her military strategy is flawless. Throughout the play, in all sorts of situations, Joan's basic honesty and her innocence shine through all of the hypocrisy of the others, and when her judges use complicated ecclesiastical terms to trap her, her basic common sense makes them look stupid. She is, however, inexperienced in the ways of the medieval society and ignorant of the jealousies of the feudal system. Her belief in the rightness of her own conscience and her refusal to yield to the authority of the Church have caused Shaw and others to refer to her as the first Protestant to be martyred by the Catholic Church.

Robert de Baudricourt

A gentlemanly squire from Joan's district, Lorraine; he is the first person of position or rank to back The Maid's plans. Through him, Joan is able to obtain her first armor and her first chance to show her military skills.

Bertrand de Poulengey (Polly)

One of Joan's first converts, he aids Joan in getting an audience with Robert de Baudricourt, and he later rides with her in the Battle of Orleans.

The Archbishop of Rheims

The churchman who, at first, sees Joan as a pious and innocent girl, one who is in close service with God. As Joan proves to be constantly right, however, and, later, when Joan is responsible for crowning the Dauphin king, the Archbishop becomes disheartened with The Maid and, ultimately, he sides against her.

Monseigneur de la Tremouille

The Lord Chamberlain in the court of the Dauphin and also the "commander-in-chief" of the French forces. He has been accustomed to bullying the Dauphin, and, therefore, he deeply resents Joan when she is given command of the French forces.

Gilles de Rais (Bluebeard)

A captain in the army and a devoted follower of The Maid, even though he is not a religious person.

The Dauphin

Later to be crowned Charles VII in the Rheims Cathedral, the Dauphin is portrayed as weak, sniveling, and unconcerned about matters of the court or of the country. He is forced by The Maid to become more manly and to assume an authority that he does not want.

Dunois (The Bastard)

The young, popular, and efficient leader of the French forces who recognizes Joan's military genius, but in the final battle is not convinced that she should be saved.

The Earl of Warwick

The English earl in charge of the English forces and Joan's most bitter and avid secular opponent. He sees Joan's simple opinions that the people should give their allegiance directly to the king as being a threat to the loyalty that the feudal lords demand from their serfs. He demands Joan's death as a way of retaining the status quo of the feudal system.

John de Stogumber

The Earl of Warwick's chaplain. At first, he is seen as a vicious and ferocious accuser of Joan's. He sees her in the most simplistic terms as a witch who should be burned without delay. He does not understand either the most complicated or the most subtle arguments concerning Joan's threat to the Church and to the aristocracy. However, the most dramatic change of the entire drama occurs in the person of de Stogumber; after he has witnessed the burning of The Maid, he becomes a weak, broken man who spends the rest of his life trying to do good deeds for others in order to alleviate his guilt for his vicious attacks against The Maid.

Peter Cauchon

The academic theologian who represents the "considered wisdom of the Church." For him, Joan represents a direct threat to the historical power invested in the Church, and he is proud that he has never asserted his own individuality and has always yielded to the opinion of the Church. For Joan to assert her own private conscience, to rely upon her own judgments, and to commune directly with God without the intervention of the Church is, to Cauchon, heresy in its highest form.

The Inquisitor

Physically, the Inquisitor should look like a kindly and sweet elderly gentleman. However, he represents the institutions of the Church in their most iron-clad disciplines. He believes strongly in the rightness of these institutions and in the collected wisdom of the Church. The individual conscience must be subjected to the authority of the Church, not just in this particular instance but throughout all time. His long rambling speech on heresy shows him to be a defender of these institutions and one who rejects any type of individualism.

D'Estivet

The Prosecutor against Joan; he is often impatient with the subtle questions of the court, and his case is based on pure legalism.

Courcelles

A young priest who has been of help in compiling some sixty-four charges against The Maid; he is incensed that many of the charges ("She stole the Bishop's horse") have been dismissed by the court.

Brother Martin Ladvenu

A sympathetic young priest who wants to save Joan's life and who is seemingly deeply concerned about Joan's inability to intellectually distinguish or understand the charges made against her. He feels her only sin is her ignorance, but once she is sentenced, he declares her imprisonment to be just. However, he holds up the cross for Joan to see while she is on her funeral stake, and he is instrumental in Joan's rehabilitation.

The Executioner

He represents the horrors of the stake. His other importance is that he reports that The Maid's heart would not burn.

An English Soldier

He is the common soldier who makes a cross out of two sticks and gives it to Joan. For this deed, he receives one day a year out of Hell.

THE PREFACE

As noted in this volume concerning *Major Barbara*, Shaw often writes a lengthy preface to his plays for his readers, in which he will comment on matters in the play or matters relevant to it. The Preface to *Saint Joan* is one of Shaw's longer ones and presents again many of his views of the personage of Joan from a more objective point of view. The Preface is divided into forty-one sub-sections which could be loosely divided into the following categories for discussion:

     (A) Sections 1-16: Various Views of the Historical Joan
     (B) Sections 17-21: Misrepresentations of Joan in Literature and
                             in Relation to Medieval Society and the
                             Medieval Church

(C) Sections 22-34: The Nature of Joan's Death in Relation to Modern Acts of Inhumanity

(D) Sections 35-41: The Nature of Historical Drama and *Saint Joan* viewed as a Tragedy

(A): Shaw sees Joan, ironically, as one of the first Protestant martyrs and as a forerunner of equality for women; Joan was burned as a heretic, thus martyred, for two primary reasons: (1) even though Joan never denied the Church and although she constantly turned to it for solace, she was, in essence, the "first Protestant" because she listened to the dictates of her own conscience and her own reasoning rather than to the authority of the Church; (2) she was "the pioneer of rational dressing for women," yet for this so-called unwomanly and, thus, *unnatural* act, she was burnt at the stake.

Joan was innocent in all things. She was like Socrates in that she was able to humiliate, without intending to do so, all kinds of people in high authority. It is extremely dangerous to publicly expose the ignorance of people in authority, and, for this, Joan and Socrates were put to death. In reality, Joan was a rather unsophisticated country girl who, while uneducated, was far from unintelligent. The fact that she could not read nor write (Marie Antoinette could not even spell her own name at Joan's age) does not matter; she did, however, manage to dictate full and comprehensive letters and to understand thoroughly the political and, especially, the military situation in France, and she had the common sense and ability to put her views in action. Since no one would believe that a simple country girl could be so talented, Joan attributed her views to "her voices and visions." To Shaw, "there are people in the world whose imagination is so vivid that when they have an idea it comes to them as an audible voice, sometimes uttered by a visible figure." Thus, Joan is able to intellectually analyze a situation so clearly that her knowledge seems, to her, to come from an outside source when, in reality, it is her own innate, unrecognized genius coming from her intelligence and imagination, tempered by her good common sense, her practical management of military affairs and her own personal courage and dedication. These are, indeed, the qualities which make for a saint. Ultimately, however, Joan's inability to fathom the complicated structure of the medieval aristocracy or the medieval Church brought about her burning.

(B): Joan has inspired others to write about her and to ascribe to her all sorts of qualities which are not always historically true, and also to interpret her actions in various ways throughout the centuries. Most of these accounts distort both Joan's life and medieval society as well. From Shakespeare through Voltaire, from Schiller to Mark Twain, and from Anatole France and others, Joan and her trials have been the source for writers to interpret her fate, according to the age in which the writer lived. None, however, have depicted her accurately; all writers are victims of their own prejudices because to understand Joan, one must understand her environment. Shaw says: ". . . to see her in her proper perspective, you must understand Christendom and the Catholic Church, the Holy Roman Empire, and the Feudal System as they existed and were understood in the Middle Ages." At that time, there were no "neutral tribunals"; therefore, neither Joan nor anyone could possibly have received an impartial trial—that is, Joan was tried *not* as a traitor to her country, but as a heretic against God and God's Church. Her judges did not recognize national boundaries, only the Universal Church, and the Church could not tolerate Joan's questioning its authority.

(C): Joan's burning at the stake was "just as dozens of less interesting heretics were burnt in her time." Shaw then cites several examples of inhumane and cruel punishments being practiced today. And even though the medieval Church would not tolerate Joan's individualism, the modern world will not tolerate a person who denounces the authority of whoever happens to be in power. The world today is no closer to accepting a genius—or a saint—than was Joan's world. Joan, had she not been captured and burned, would probably have driven the English out of France, and then would have retired quietly to her country home. However, "the real Joan [has never been] marvelous enough for us," and, therefore, writers have often altered the facts of her life for their own purposes.

(D): The problems and the "stage limits" of writing a historical play are numerous. Shaw compares Shakespeare's methods and efforts of writing historical dramas with his own. Actually, Shakespeare never attempted to deal with the larger forces of the law and religion and patriotism that cause men to act as they do. Shaw has one advantage over other, earlier writers: he is, chronologically, further away and, therefore, is able to have a more complete view of the Middle Ages. Shaw also maintains that his play is a tragedy, not a melodrama; there are no villains in *Saint Joan*, only characters caught in their historical period. Likewise, the Epilogue is necessary even though it is not historical. If the play showed Joan burned at the stake, then an Epilogue is needed to show her canonized and, more important, to present a balance between "the tragedy of her execution" and "the comedy of the attempts of posterity to make amends."

CRITICAL COMMENTARIES

SCENE I

Summary

The scene takes place in the spring of the year 1429 A.D. in the castle of Captain Robert de Baudricourt, a "handsome and physically energetic" man with "no will of his own." Sir Robert is blustering about because there are no eggs. His steward maintains that it is an "act of God," and that the hens will not lay because "there is a spell on us: we are bewitched . . . as long as The Maid is at the door." Sir Robert is thunderstruck that The Maid from Lorraine is still outside because he dismissed her two days ago, but we hear that she will not leave ("she is so positive") until Sir Robert grants her an interview. In a blustering manner, he goes to the window and orders her to come up.

When Joan enters, she is seen to be a sixteen- or seventeen-year-old able-bodied country girl. She immediately informs Sir Robert that he is *ordered* to give her a horse, armor, and some soldiers, and that he must send her to the Dauphin. Sir Robert is offended that anyone would dare to give him orders, and he is astonished to find out that the "lord" who sent the orders is the "Lord of Heaven." He immediately assumes that the girl is mad. She then tells him exactly the costs of the armor and the horses and that she will not need many soldiers because the Dauphin will provide her with enough soldiers to "raise the siege of Orleans." The voices of Saints Catherine and Margaret have spoken to her and told her that this is to be so. Furthermore, she lets Sir Robert know that some of his noblemen, such as Bertrand de Poulengey (Polly) is anxious to go with her. Hearing this, Sir Robert dismisses The Maid and sends for "Polly."

Sir Robert first chastises Polly about a possible sexual liaison, but he is completely assured that nothing of the sort exists. Nevertheless,

The Maid, states Sir Robert, is a "country girl," a "bourgeoise," and is apparently mad. Poulengey, however, reviews the military position: the English (along with their French allies, the Burgundians) hold over half of France; the Dauphin is trapped "like a rat in a corner" and does nothing; even The Bastard (Dunois) cannot save Orleans; thus, what is needed is a miracle: as Poulengey says, "We want a few mad people now. See where the sane ones have landed us!" When Poulengey volunteers to pay for the horse, Sir Robert begins to waver and thus he sends once more for The Maid.

When questioned, Joan maintains that she is following the instructions of her "voices" (which she will not further discuss) which tell her that the English "are only men" and that they must be forced to return to "their own country and their own language." She asserts that Sir Robert *will* live to see the day "when there will not be an English soldier on the soil of France" and when there will be one king – "God's French one."

Sir Robert is finally convinced; he believes that the troops and, ultimately, the Dauphin "might swallow" Joan's conviction and her dedication; maybe even the Dauphin might take courage from Joan's determination. At least, it is worth a try. He thus orders Joan to go to Chinon under Poulengey's escort; she is given a soldier's armor, and she dashes off ecstatically. Sir Robert then admits that "There is *something* about her." The scene ends with the hens "laying like mad."

Commentary

In the opening scene, some very important aspects of Joan's character are revealed. First, she is seen as a strong-willed person who goes straight to the heart of matters. In contrast, Sir Robert de Baudricourt is described as a person "with no will of his own"; thus, this opening scene shows Joan being able to firmly assert her own will in a direct, forthright, and candid manner. In other words, Joan is an iron-willed woman who very easily dominates Sir Robert, who is seen as a man of many doubts and no strong convictions. As the Steward says of Joan: "Sir, she *is* so positive." Second, immediately after Joan speaks of her mission as being from God, Sir Robert immediately declares her to be mad. Thus, until her death, the matter of Joan's voices are connected with her sanity and will, of course, become the instrument of her death at the stake. Furthermore, Joan's seeming connections with the supernatural is seen in a rather comic (melodramatic) use of Sir Robert's hens not laying eggs until The Maid has her way. Also, in the discussion between Sir Robert and Polly, we are told that sex has no part in The Maid's demeanor. Since many of Joan's detractors have insinuated a sexual attraction and since, later on, Joan is accused of sexual perversion by wearing men's clothes, Shaw immediately let us know that *his* Joan does not rely upon sex for her basic appeal. In contrast, Shaw's Joan is essentially asexual throughout the drama.

The subject of miracles is also introduced. A saint is one who is most often associated with a miracle of some sort, and when the situation in France is evaluated, then only a miracle can save France. But, again, the question of Joan's sanity is raised. The irony here is that a saint, by very definition, is not a *normal* person – a saint is indeed an exceptional (or abnormal) person. Thus, Shaw is very careful to introduce many of his main themes into this first scene. For example, Joan is later to be tried and condemned upon the validity of the "voices" which she hears, and, here, Sir Robert introduces the first skepticism about the voices:

JOAN: . . . you must not talk to me about my voices.
ROBERT: How do you mean? Voices?
JOAN: I hear voices telling me what to do. They come from God.
ROBERT: They come from your imagination.

Consequently, Joan must be abnormal: she is a country girl of seventeen who hears voices which tell her to shed her female clothing and live with and lead an army of men against the powerful English forces. Her duty is, thus, to drive the English out by uniting the French forces which, until now, have lacked discipline, direction, and inspired leadership. It is this very inspiration which will ultimately make Joan so successful – even though later it is often iterated that she could instinctively grasp battle tactics and strategic placements of artillery. At the end of the scene, even Sir Robert takes up the general statement, "There is *something* about her."

Theatrically, Shaw opens and closes the scene with the melodramatic device of the absurd pseudo-miracle of the eggs. This is ultimately a true comment because most people, once convinced that a person is a saint, will then attribute all sorts of "miracles" to the person.

SCENE II

Summary

The scene is set in the antechamber of the throne room of the Dauphin's castle in Chinon. The Archbishop of Rheims and la Trémouille are discussing the huge sums of money that the Dauphin has borrowed from them, and yet the Dauphin is still on the verge of poverty when young Gilles de Rais, better known as Bluebeard, enters and reports that The Maid has had a tremendous effect on the common soldiers; this is confirmed by Captain La Hire, who believes that Joan must be "an angel dressed as a soldier," especially since she has overcome impossible odds, even to get to Chinon.

The Dauphin, twenty-six years old, enters with a letter about Joan from Sir Robert de Baudricourt, a letter which is bandied about as the Archbishop and the Chamberlain (la Tremouille) bully and intimidate the Dauphin, refusing to let him see The Maid, especially since she is *not* a respectable person. After some more arguing, Bluebeard offers a challenge: he will pretend to be the Dauphin, and if The Maid cannot distinguish royalty from common blood, then she is a pretender; if she can, then she must be heaven-sent. They all then argue about the siege of Orleans and why the highly touted, respected, and beloved Bastard, Dunois, cannot do anything with his military forces. It is agreed that a miracle is indeed needed. When Bluebeard and the Dauphin leave to prepare for the impersonation, the Archbishop and the Chamberlain discuss the nature of miracles. For the Archbishop, a miracle is any "event which creates faith." Furthermore, the Archbishop asserts that the Church alone must decide what is good for the souls of men: ". . . the Church must . . . nourish their faith by poetry." Thus, when The Maid correctly ferrets out the hidden Dauphin, the Archbishop will know how it is done, but if the others think it is a miracle, then let that be their thrill.

The curtains to the antechamber are drawn, revealing the full depth of the throne room, with various members of the royal court assembled. Joan, dressed as a soldier, and with cropped hair, is admitted, and she creates an immediate sense of hilarity among the ladies because of her attire. Joan, however, is not at all embarrassed, and when Bluebeard tries to deceive her, she readily dismisses him and goes into the crowd to discover the Dauphin. She drags him from the crowd and tells him that she has been sent to free France of the English and to crown him king in the Cathedral at Rheims. When the Archbishop is consulted on this matter, he is soon convinced that Joan is indeed pious, and he asks everyone to leave The Maid alone with the Dauphin.

Alone, Charles (the Dauphin) confesses his fright and his miserable condition. The others enjoy fighting. On the contrary, however, Charles is "quiet and sensible," and he doesn't "want to kill people." He simply wishes to be left alone to live peacefully. Joan counters that she will "put courage into thee," even though the Dauphin doesn't want courage; he wants to sleep in a comfortable bed and not live in continual terror of being killed or wounded. Charles wants Joan to mind her own business and let him mind his. Joan, however, gradually begins to instill courage and patriotism in him as she tells him forcefully that she will crown him king in Rheims. In resounding rhetoric, Joan promises him that the English will be defeated and France will become holy and the Dauphin will rule. Suddenly, inspired by Joan's faith and enthusiasm, the Dauphin recalls the members of his court and announces that he has given command of the army to The Maid to do with as she likes. As the Chamberlain moves threateningly forward, asserting that *he* is the commander of the army, Joan pushes the frightened Dauphin forward. He snaps his finger in the Chamberlain's face as Joan draws her sword, kneels, and cries out: "Who is for God and His Maid? Who is for Orleans with me?" All of the knights draw their swords in support of The Maid, as the Archbishop gives a sign of blessing to all gathered here.

Commentary

Again, the "supernatural" aspect of Joan's character is emphasized in the miraculous changes which she has wrought among the common soldiers, even causing the most hardened soldiers to give up their cursing until La Hire believes her to be an "angel dressed as a soldier." The view of the common people toward Joan will never waver, and in the Epilogue, we find out that the common people adored her in spite of the Church's condemnation. One essential objection to Joan is again stated by the Archbishop when he maintains that she is not a *respectable* woman because "she does not wear women's clothes," and, thus, she is "unwomanly." The issue of Joan's clothes will become central to her trial and will play a significant part in her condemnation. But of larger importance, *war has always been the business of men;* this is the announced theme of Homer's *Iliad* and of Virgil's *Aeneid,* and here, we have a young country girl of seventeen usurping the perogatives of mature, experienced soldiers, but then, the Dauphin is no "manly" man – that is, he needs someone to order him about, as Joan will do.

When the Archbishop, in discussing miracles, maintains that a miracle is any event which creates faith, he has unintentionally described Joan's entire life and her actions; yet this view is completely overlooked at her trial when all of her accomplishments are debunked.

The first two scenes function as studies in contrast. Whereas Sir Robert de Baudricourt possesses great enthusiasm, yet lacks a basic understanding of the nature of martial affairs, the courtiers, on the other hand, have a complete and total perception of what needs to be done, but they have no dedication, no spirit. They are rendered into inertia; they are paralyzed by their own self-interest. This is best seen through the Dauphin, who detests war, who wants to be left alone, and who resents the idea that he was born into kingship. Thus, the fact that Joan can inspire such an insipid person attests to her "miraculous" powers of persuasion and leadership.

Finally, this scene introduces part of the rationale by which Joan is ultimately condemned to the stake. In a theological sense, Joan will ultimately be condemned because she prefers to obey her inner voices rather than obey the authority of the Church. In this scene, the Archbishop introduces the idea that "the Church has to rule for the good of their souls . . . the Church must . . . nourish their faith by poetry." In other words, the individual must *always* yield to the authority of the Church, and Joan is the epitome of the Protestants who prefer to believe in their own consciences rather than in the Church's authority.

SCENE III

Summary

This scene is set on the south bank of the Loire River, near Orleans, about seven weeks later. Dunois, better known as The Bastard, is seen pacing up and down the river bank, calling on the west wind to blow in his direction, for he constantly observes his pennon (the flag on his lance) blowing the wrong way. A page enters, and Dunois immediately inquires as to the whereabouts of The Maid, who suddenly arrives in full armor. Immediately, the west wind stops blowing, but Dunois is too occupied to notice. Upon identifying Dunois as "The Bastard of Orleans," Joan wonders why they are on *this* side of the river when the English and Orleans are on the other side. She wants to cross the bridge immediately and attack the English forces. Dunois explains that older and wiser military experts say such a tactic simply cannot be done, but Joan dismisses the experts as "fatheads"; she is determined to take immediate, decisive action. When Dunois mentions that her soldiers will not follow her into the mouth of almost certain death, she asserts: "I will not look back to see whether anyone is following me." She then informs Dunois that she will charge the fort and will be the first up the ladder and she dares him to follow her. Dunois responds that they must sail *up* river and attack the English from the rear, but, first, they "must wait until God changes the wind." He then asks Joan to go to church and pray for an east wind. They leave to find a church, but, suddenly, the page notices that the wind has changed, and he calls The Maid and The Bastard back. Dunois thinks that God has indeed spoken, and thus he says that if Joan will lead the armies, he will pledge his allegiance to her.

Commentary

In this short scene, Dunois is presented as the darling, romantic hero whose opening speech on the west wind characterizes him as a Soldier Poet. He will make a fitting complement to The Maid, Joan. As a romantic, Dunois thinks that Joan is "in love with war"; earlier, the Archbishop had said that Joan was in love with religion. In reality, Joan is in love with neither; she is simply following her dedication (or her voices). The greatness of Joan is shown in this scene in the simple but moving manner by which she is able to convert such seasoned soldiers as Dunois, who is, of course, the realistic soldier who evaluates the tactical difficulties of the situation before moving into action. Joan, in contrast, moves immediately – by inspiration.

This scene also continues with the miraculous nature of Joan's presence. Here, the miracle involves the changing of the wind. Since Dunois has waited for so long for the wind to change and then, suddenly, realizes that it has reversed itself at the very moment that Joan is about to attack, this is proof enough for Dunois that Joan possesses miraculous powers. Therefore, Joan becomes a force like the west wind; in other words, Joan moves forward toward her goal, unconscious of the larger implications. She is simply "blown" toward victory.

SCENE IV

Summary

This scene is set in the English camp, as the nobleman Richard de Beauchamp, Earl of Warwick (called simply Warwick) discusses the recent series of unbelievable French victories with his chaplain, de Stogumber. The defeats can be accounted for only by "witchcraft and sorcery." No simple girl could *possibly* have defeated the English forces unless she were "an accursed witch." Warwick reveals that he is ready to pay a large ransom for the witch so as to burn her.

A page announces the arrival of the Bishop of Beauvais, Peter Cauchon. After Warwick acknowledges that The Maid has now arranged to have Charles crowned at Rheims and that the English are helpless, Warwick offers his view that The Maid is a sorceress who should be denounced to the Inquisition.

De Stogumber is more adamant in his condemnation, citing the numerous victories which Joan has had over the English and her miraculous survivals on the battlefield. Cauchon is not wholly convinced that the French victories were caused by witchcraft: he subtly suggests that some "little of the credit" be given to French leadership, and he cites examples. However, he agrees that The Maid has supernatural powers, but he attributes these powers to the Devil; the Devil, he says, is employing Joan to strike at the very basis of the Catholic Church: ". . . it is as one of the instruments of that design that . . . this girl is inspired, but diabolically inspired." Thus, Joan is *not* a witch, but, instead, she is a *heretic*. Cauchon does not believe her accomplishments (her victories) to be miracles, but simply that Joan "has a better head on her shoulders" than do the blustering English generals whom she has defeated. However, it is the duty of the Church to save souls, which Cauchon hopes to do: "The soul of this village girl is of equal value with yours or your king's before the throne of God; and my first duty is to save it."

Cauchon, then, in a long diatribe, explains Joan's condemnation. Joan, he says, totally ignores the Church and, furthermore, she *presumes* to bring messages directly from God; likewise, she, and not the Church, will crown Charles. All of her actions are performed without consulting the Church; in short, she acts as though she *were* the Church, This is heresy in its worst form and, Cauchon says, it must be "stamped out, burnt out." Cauchon then catalogues a history of heretics from Mahomet down to Joan – heretics, he says, because they listened to their own personal voices and visions instead of listening to the collected wisdom of the Church. What would happen to the Church if all individuals listened to their own consciences rather than to the Church? Cauchon vows to destroy all such heretics.

Warwick, however, is not impressed by these theological arguments. He is not frightened that Joan might become another Mahomet and create another great schism in the Church; instead, he sees a greater danger, one that involves the very basis of the social structure of all Europe. Joan's views would do away with the feudal hierarchy of the aristocracy, a system in which the king is merely first among his peers and she would, instead, create a system in which the king would be responsible to God, ruling "as God's bailiff" and dismissing the rest of the nobility. Under this system, all of the nobility would have to surrender their lands to the king, who would then present them to God (the Church); thus, the king would be ruled by the Church. In addition, the power of the feudal lords now comes from the allegiance of the common people; Joan's new system of social reform would shift that allegiance from the feudal lord *directly* to the king, leaving the lords without any power. Interestingly, Cauchon, as a churchman, does *not* find this idea unacceptable.

Cauchon sees that Warwick is not concerned with Joan's effect on the Church, but only with the nobility, yet he listens as Warwick points out that Joan's ideas about the peerage (the nobility) and the Church are, to Warwick, basically identical. In both cases, Warwick says, Joan would do away with any person that stood between the average person and that person's allegiance to his God or to his king: "It is the protest of the individual soul against the interference of priest or peer between the private man and his God." Warwick labels this as "Protestantism." Cauchon then extends the analogy to something which he calls "Nationalism." That is, The Maid is trying to instill a sense of national pride into the common people toward their national origins: "France for the French, England for the English, Italy for the Italians . . . and so forth"; this is contrary to the current state of affairs in which the Church's rule is a universal rule – one realm – one kingdom of Christ—and not several divided nations with different rulers and different allegiances.

De Stogumber has been thoroughly confused by this discussion of "Protestant and Nationalist" and simply says that The Maid rebels against Nature (by wearing men's clothes), against the Church (by listening to her voices instead of the Church's), and against God (by aligning herself with Satan in witchcraft). Even though de Stogumber has missed the crux of Warwick's and Couchon's arguments, all agree that The Maid must "die for the people."

Commentary

Shaw once said that *Saint Joan*, as a drama, begins with this fourth scene, and that the early scenes were merely "theater." Shaw's statements, of course, must always be taken both seriously *and* skeptically. As theater, the first three scenes are absolutely essential to setting up the dramatic conflicts on the most basic level. But with this scene, the more complex drama of ideas is introduced, and the conflicts from here to the end of the drama will be the dramatic confrontations of different ideas.

Basically, in this scene, Shaw is again emphasizing Joan's supernatural tendencies. For de Stogumber (who is called a simpleton because the entire discussion about Protestantism and Nationalism is over his head and the final words of the Bishop is to bless de Stogumber as a simpleton: "Sancta simplicitas!"), the English have been defeated over and over again in battles, and thus he can only assume that their defeats are due to the witchcraft of The Maid. The more people who cry 'Witch,' and the more often the cry is repeated, then the more often it will be believed without judging the validity of the accusation. And it should be firmly noted that Bishop Cauchon does *not* believe that Joan *is* a witch; instead, he believes that Joan is something much more dangerous, theologically—that is, she is a *heretic*.

In reading a drama of ideas, such as *Saint Joan*, an accurate summary of the action is, in itself, a comment or explanation of the meaning of the play. After all, the essence of this act is found in the philosophical, theological and sociological debate between the representative of the peerage (Warwick) and the representative of the Church (Cauchon). Thus, their arguments (or the argumentation) between them become the dramatic action of this scene, and it is for this reason that Shaw slyly calls this scene the real begining of *Saint Joan*.

To restate the arguments as Shaw presents them: Warwick represents the argument for all of the feudal lords – that is, he, Warwick, is the representative for medieval political and social feudalism. In other words, the feudal system was based upon the common people pledging their total allegiance to their immediate lords and then the lords would, in turn, deal with the king. Joan, however, is espousing a concept that the common people should pledge their allegiance directly to the king, thus threatening the existence of the feudal lords. Thus, Warwick, as the representative of feudalism, wants The Maid destroyed so as to preserve the status quo of the feudal system. In other words, it is either destroy Joan the Maid, or have Warwick's social system be destroyed by her.

Likewise, Cauchon is the representative of the Universal Church, and the heirarchy of the Church is on a parallel with that of the feudal lords (in medieval times, they were referred to as the *Lords Spiritual* and the *Lords Temporal*). As a bishop in the Church, Cauchon interprets for the common people – that is, he acts as an intercessory between the people and God. If The Maid has her way, then the common people would be able to talk directly to God and would therefore render the Church useless. Furthermore, if The Maid has her way, the common people would begin to give their allegiance to *nations* – rather than yielding themselves to the Universal Church; once allegiances are split, then the Church loses much of its power.

The irony here is that neither Cauchon nor Warwick is sympathetic for the other's reasons for wanting Joan destroyed, but since Joan represents a threat to both the existence of feudalism and to the authority of the Church, they both agree, separately, that she must be destroyed. On the comic level, de Stogumber simply wants her destroyed without understanding *any* of the philosophical reasons for the necessity of her death.

SCENE V

Summary

This scene is set inside the door of the Cathedral at Rheims, where the Dauphin has just been coronated King Charles VII. Joan is seen kneeling before one of the 'stations of the cross.' Denois enters, hoping to bring Joan outside and present her to the masses who are calling for her, but Joan says that she wants Charles, the new king "to have all the glory." In a discussion between them, Dunois reveals that Joan, while adored by the common soldiers and the masses, does not have many friends at Court. When Joan fails to comprehend the Court's animosity toward her, Dunois explains that she has constantly proven herself superior to important and influential men, and now she, and not the Archbishop, is responsible for crowning Charles; these important personages resent being revealed as incompetent. If this be the case, Joan says, she will return to her farm after she has taken Paris. When Dunois warns her that many would prefer that Paris (that is, the enemy) would take her, Joan explains that it is this type of wickedness which makes her rely on her voices, which gives her the confidence to keep going. Her discussion of her voices tends to unnerve Dunois, who would think that she were crazy were it not for her very sensible and logical reasons for her battle strategy.

Bluebeard and La Hire enter as Charles complains about the weight of his coronation robes and the rancid smell of the holy oil. When he hears that The Maid plans to return home, he is greatly pleased which, in turn, discourages Joan. As she is talking with the others, she suddenly tells Dunois: "Before I go home, let's take Paris." This deeply distresses and horrifies the King, who wants an immediate treaty and *no more fighting*. As Joan becomes impatient with the King, the Archbishop enters and tries to restrain Joan's impetuosity. When Joan speaks rather sharply to the Archbishop, he reprimands her for disregarding the authority of the Church and for having clothed herself in the "sin of pride," inviting just punishment for her excessive pride. Joan asserts that her voices are her own authority, and she recalls the many triumphs which she has effected. She asserts simply: "You don't know how to begin a battle, and you don't know how to use your cannons. And I do."

Dunois interrupts to acknowledge that while God was on her side earlier, the time of miracles is now over; it is now time to rely on military experience. Furthermore, Joan never concerns herself with costs, supplies, and manpower. Dunois then points out that if Joan is captured, there is no one who will come forward to ransom or rescue her, that even he himself will not sacrifice one soldier's life for her, but she asserts that France (that is, the Crown) will ransom her. Charles immediately denies this, especially since expenses of this dreadful coronation which she forced on him have taken his last cent. When she puts her trust in the Church to aid her, the Archbishop warns her that "they will drag you through the streets and burn you as a witch," that Peter Cauchon knows his business of convicting a heretic. Joan is dumbfounded. She has acted only as God has instructed her to act; she cannot believe that the Church will not protect her now. When the Archbishop accuses her of being "proud and disobedient," Joan protests, asking how she could be disobedient when she has faithfully *obeyed* her voices—the voices that "come from God." When the Archbishop asserts that the "voices" are only the "echoes of your own willfulness," Joan simply points out one basic truth: her voices have *always* been *right*, and all of her earthly counsels have *always* been *wrong*. The Archbishop ignores this fact and gives her a last warning: if Joan continues to follow her judgment rather than the Church's, she will be disowned by the Church (the Archbishop), by the Crown (King Charles), and by the Army (Dunois): "You will stand alone: absolutely alone."

Joan then confronts her earthly compatriots and plaintively she cries out that she has always been alone on this earth—in the same way that France is alone and bleeding, and in the same way that God Himself is alone. She hoped to find friends of God in the court of France because God is a friend of everyone, but she now knows that as the loneliness of God is His strength, so too, shall her loneliness be her strength. In God's name, she says, she now has the strength to confront the enemy until she dies. She will go to the common people who love her and, there, she will gain enough strength from their love to comfort her for the hatred which these men of power hold for her; then, if she is indeed burnt at the stake, she will go through the fire to the hearts of the common people for ever and ever. She departs, saying: "God be with me."

At first, all are silenced; then Bluebeard remarks that The Maid is "quite impossible." Dunois says that, personally, he would jump into a river fully armored to rescue her, but if she were caught by the enemy in a foolish campaign, he would "leave her to her doom." La Hire, however, is inspired to follow her—even to Hell. The Archbishop is disturbed in his judgment, and Charles wishes only that Joan would be quiet and go home.

Commentary

After Scene Four set up the intellectual ideas and forces working against Joan, Scene Five returns to the personage of Joan herself and presents her at the decisive turning point in her life – her determination to rely upon the authority of her voices rather than accept the authority of the Church and the other earthly advisers or counselors.

In the opening of this scene, we see Joan refusing to accept the accolades of the crowd and, instead, being submissive and praying for guidance. When Dunois speaks of Joan's enemies, we see into the mind of a genius who is unable to comprehend the animosity which others feel toward her – especially since she is simply trying to help them. Like Socrates of ancient Greece who questioned people so as to show them their ignorance and was thus resented and put to death, so Joan cannot understand it when the people whom she has helped now resent her help; even after Dunois explains to Joan that most people do not like to be shown up as being incompetent, she cannot comprehend other people's hatred for her. Joan, in her innocence, has done only what is good for France. But note that even her strongest defender is troubled when Joan speaks of her "voices"; she can only justify the voices because, through them, she is able to give perfectly logical reasons for her many victories. She has proven over and over again to be a better general on the battlefield than is the most experienced professional, but then she states simply, "You don't know how to begin a battle and I do, and you don't know how to use your cannons. And I do." This is a simple statement of fact, but the Archbishop interprets this to be a sin of excessive pride (or the Greek *hubris*), and the others condemn her for this type of statement. They refuse to acknowledge that Joan has superior military acumen.

Shaw, in emphasizing Joan's sin as being a sin of *hubris*, as the Archbishop constantly reiterates, seems to be implying that Joan is of the stature of the ancient Greek subjects of tragedy, people such as Oedipus, or Agamemnon, and others. And whereas such great tragic figures as Oedipus and Hamlet had to stand alone against overwhelming odds, thus Joan too knows that she must now stand alone. Her refusal to listen to the earthly counsels (which have always been wrong) and her insistence upon listening to her own private voices (which have always been right) cut her off from France, from the Church, and from the Army. Whereas the Archbishop and others see her as proud and disobedient, yet her pride lies in the fact that she believes absolutely in her voices and in the very common-sensical reality of her own victories. As she told Dunois earlier, her voices come to her as a sort of poetry through the bells of the churches at times when she is silent and receptive to the voices; likewise, they could come to others if only others would also be receptive to them. In this point, Joan is the true mystic, believing that what is mystic to herself is available to everyone – if only they would be receptive.

In her powerful and climactic speech on being alone and on the subject of loneliness itself, Joan realizes that her responsibility is to a higher power than is represented by any of these earthly counselors. As is always the case with the genuine saint, Joan realizes that she is "alone on earth." In asserting her aloneness, Joan has now cut herself off from all of the powers of France, and she must now stand alone, with only the love of the common people to give her strength.

SCENE VI

Summary

This scene is set in a great hall arranged for a trial, with a circular table surrounding a rough wooden stool for the prisoner. Approximately nine months have elapsed since Joan's capture and, as we learn later, Warwick has ransomed Joan from her captors and has turned her over to the ecclesiastical court to be tried for heresy. Warwick, who is forbidden to be present at an ecclesiastical trial, has come to inquire of "Pious Peter" Cauchon about the progress of the trial. The court has already held six public and nine private examinations, and there seems to be no progress. Cauchon introduces Warwick to the Inquisitor (Brother John Lemaître), a seemingly mild, elderly man, and to the chief prosecutor, Canon John D'Estivet. The Inquisitor informs Warwick that all evidence is in, and they are ready to proceed. Warwick is informed that all that is desired by Joan's judges is to save her soul, but he demands Joan's death as a political necessity; ironically, The Maid herself is her own worst enemy: every time she speaks, she convicts herself with blasphemies.

As Warwick departs, the court assembles. De Stogumber and Canon de Courcelles protest to the court that their sixty-four meticulously drawn-up charges have been reduced to only twelve indictments. The Inquisitor, backed by Cauchon, explains that the court is not interested in "trumpery issues." The "great main issue" is heresy, and all of the wild, silly accusations about magic serve only to confuse the issues.

At this point, a young priest, Ladvenu, wonders if Joan's heresy is due only to her simplicity. The Inquisitor answers in the longest speech in the drama, asserting that heresy often begins with simple people who are often generous, lovable, humble, and charitable, people who are "saintly simpletons"; heresy, he says, begins when a simple woman rejects her clothes for the dress of a man and continues until this "vain and ignorant person" sets up her own judgment against that of the Church and attempts to interpret God's will, believing always "honestly and sincerely that [her] diabolical inspiration is divine." Furthermore, The Maid is pious and chaste, but "diabolical pride and natural humility are side by side in her." He admonishes her judges that they must avoid being either too cruel or too sympathetic toward her: "Remember only that justice comes first." Cauchon agrees with the Inquisitor, and he reminds the court of the great danger called "Protestantism," in which private individuals set up their own private judgments against the collected wisdom of the Church, thus threatening the "mighty structure of Catholic Christendom."

Joan is brought in, chained by the ankles and showing the strain of the long imprisonment and harsh treatment. She is immediately attacked on some minor points by Prosecutor D'Estivet. When Joan balks at swearing to tell the truth once more (for the tenth time), she is threatened with physical torture. After more time is wasted on trifles, Bishop Cauchon then asks Joan the essential question: "Will you submit your case to the inspired intrepretation of the Church Militant?" Joan agrees to obey the Church *only* if it does not ask her to deny the heavenly origin of her voices; furthermore, if the Church bids her to do something contrary to God's command, she cannot consent. This assertion causes extreme consternation among her accusers, who consider it heresy to even think that the Church *could* suggest something contrary to God.

When Ladvenu pleads with Joan to accept the authority of the Church, Joan maintains that she has never disobeyed the Church, only that God must be served first, and she believes herself to be in a state of grace with God. Courcelles wonders if this was so when she stole the Bishop's horse, a silly question which causes disorder in the court. D'Estivet then charges Joan with having "intercourse with evil spirits" and of dressing like a soldier. Joan defends her voices as heavenly voices, and she explains impatiently the necessity of her dress in plain common sense terms: it would be foolish to live among soldiers while dressed as a woman, and, furthermore, in an enemy prison, it would be even more foolhardy to wear petticoats. As Joan continues to make impatient and pert or sarcastic replies, she is reminded that the Executioner is standing directly behind her, a man who confirms that the stake is ready for Joan's immediate burning. Joan finds herself in desperate despair: she is terrified of burning at the stake, but she asserts that her voices promised her that she should not be burnt. Ladvenu and Cauchon use her fears to make her confess that her voices have betrayed her: she finally agrees that her voices have deceived her because "only a fool will walk into a fire"; God would not expect her to go to the stake. Her judges are triumphant and immediately bring her "a solemn recantation of heresy" to sign. De Stogumber interrupts the proceedings and denounces the court, asserting that eight hundred Englishmen wait outside, ready to burn The Maid. When de Stogumber is quieted, Ladvenu reads to Joan the recantation which renounces her voices as false and states that she embraces the Church for bringing her to salvation, and, in addition, that she pledges *total allegiance* to the authority of the Church. Ladvenu guides her hand to sign the document, and Joan is pronounced free from the danger of excommunication, *but* because she has sinned most presumptuously, she is sentenced to spend the rest of her life in solitary confinement and perpetual imprisonment, living on only bread and water.

Upon hearing her sentence, Joan immediately denounces the recantation document, dreading imprisonment in a rat-infested hole more than the flames of the stake. She tears her confession to shreds and denounces the assembled court as fools. She cries out that she is not frightened of bread and water, but only of being shut away in darkness, of being denied the light of the sky, the sights of the fields; living in chains forever, she says, is impossible. To keep her from the very forces of life is the counsel of the Devil, for she, she states, is keeping God's counsel. She pronounces the court to be unfit for her to live among them. The Inquisitor and Cauchon immediately pronounce her "a relapsed heretic," and they state that she must be cast out and abandoned. Joan is brutally hurried to the stake, followed by Ladvenu, who will be by her side for her last confession. When the flames can be seen inside, Cauchon says that he wants to stop the burning because of some technical irregularities, but the Inquisitor stops him, explaining that the Church proceeded in perfect order, and it is the English who are guilty of irregularities. This fact might be useful in the future because of the innocence of The Maid. The Inquisitor then explains that Joan was innocent because she understood nothing about the proceedings; she was merely crushed by the Church and the Law.

As the Inquisitor and Cauchon leave to witness the burning, Warwick enters and is soon followed by de Stogumber, who staggers like a demented person to the prisoner's stool and sobs uncontrollably. When asked what the matter is, he blubbers out that he did not know what he was doing and did not know how horrible death by burning was. He is thankful that The Maid asked for a cross because an English soldier was able to give her two sticks tied together for her final consolation. De Stogumber says that he feels that he is damned, and he is admonished to control himself just as Ladvenu enters, carrying a cross which he held for The Maid to see during her last moments of life; he says that he climbed onto the burning pyre, but that Joan sent him back, admonishing him of the danger to himself. Ladvenu cannot understand how Joan could, at such a time, think of the safety of others unless she were with God.

When de Stogumber rushes out to pray among Joan's ashes, Warwick sends Ladvenu to look after the Chaplain. Then, unexpectedly, the Executioner comes to report that the execution is complete. Warwick wants assurance that no relics remain that could be sold; the Executioner, however, reports that Joan's *heart* would not burn, but that all the rest of her remains are at the bottom of a river. When verbally assured that he has heard the last of The Maid, Warwick, with a wry smile, wonders if he has truly heard the last of Joan of Arc.

Commentary

The very setting of this scene is intensely dramatic. Joan is placed on a rough wooden stool surrounded by her adversaries – with no one to defend her except herself and her innocence; her denial of a defense counsel is a contradiction of modern law, and, of particular note here is the fact that all representatives of the Church maintain that she needs no defense because they *all* want to save her soul; this statement and all like it must be viewed as cruelly ironical and hypocritical because after Joan is convicted, the Inquisitor acknowledges that she was completely innocent. Likewise, the title "saint" in the play's title, as well as Joan's subsequent rehabilitation, put the audiences completely on Joan's side against the Prosecutor. Of course, the Inquisitor knows from the beginning that Joan is innocent. *This is Shaw's point.* As with Warwick, who knows that Joan has not deliberately plotted to destroy the feudal system, but that her innocent statements are damning and that The Maid must die for political reasons, the Inquisitor also knows that Joan's innocence is more dangerous than any calculated plot against the Church itself. *But,* if the Church allowed people to follow their own simple consciences and their innocent instincts, feelings that "seemingly" come directly from God, then the entire structure of the Church would be undermined. Joan, in her innocence, has no desire to destroy the Church, but in following the purity of her own voices (that is, her own conscience), she becomes the greatest possible threat to the authority of the Church – for if everyone followed the dictates of their own conscience, then the entire structure of the Church would collapse. Consequently, the beginning of Joan's entire damnation occurs when the Church's representatives ask her if she will forgo her own opinions (her voices) and accept the judgments of the Church as completely authoritative.

The Inquisitor, in his long speech, points out that great heresies occur when simple, innocent people like Joan begin to trust in their own consciences rather than listen to the authority of the Church. The Church can exist only when it has *total* authority, and it must stamp out any dissent or "Protestantism." The existence of the Church is more important than the life of a simple country maid. If Joan is allowed to live, then other, also innocent country people might begin to trust their own personal judgments and ignore the Church's interpretations and authority. Consequently, Joan must die for the sake of preserving the status quo of the feudal system of the authority of the Church. Anyone, however innocent, must die if that person tries to set up "the private judgment of the single erring mortal against the considered wisdom and experience of the Church." Consequently, as the Inquisitor points out, Joan in her innocence constantly condemns herself, especially in such statements as the following: "In case the Church should bid me to do anything contrary to the command I have from God, I will not consent to it, no matter what it may be."

This statement is enough to hang her since she has openly asserted that the Church might indeed suggest something contrary to God, and the further implication is that Joan, a simple maid, can interpret God's message better than can the Church. This is indeed "Protestantism."

Dramatically, Shaw plays off his simple spokesman for Truth against his crafty, ambiguous characterizations of the representatives of the Church. For example, the Inquisitor is presented as a kindly old gentleman who professes a deep concern over the personal welfare of The Maid. But behind the Inquisitor's facade is an iron mind which knows that Joan is innocent, that she is *not* in league with the Devil, and that her failure to intellectually understand the charges will condemn her in spite of her innocence. But like Warwick, the Inquisitor knows that Joan must be sacrificed for the sake of the authority of the Church. Thus, behind the kindly facade is the determined mind of the Executioner. Likewise, the greatest dramatic change occurs in the character of de Stogumber. In earlier scenes, as well as here, de Stogumber is presented as a comic figure. His ferocity in demanding that The Maid be convicted and burnt as a witch is therefore dramatically contrasted to the change in his character after witnessing the actual burning of The Maid; now, his early ferocity and hatred turn inward upon him, and we see him ultimately as a repentant, sobbing hysterical man.

Throughout Joan's testimony, in addition to her common sense, her gentle faith, her innocence, her simplicity, and her transcendent beauty shine through the depressing Inquisition as though it were her saintly halo. Indeed, throughout the entire scene, Joan is seen as a person of great common sense, a person whose answers are so incontrovertible that it makes her questioners seem like fools. Yet even though Joan is right when she tells D'Estivet, "Nobody could be such a fool as to believe . . ." what he has just told her, yet her very answer suggests that she has not the proper respect for the authority of the Church, even though the questions of the Church are stupid and foolish. Her explanation about the nature of her dress (one should not dress in feminine finery when one is being guarded by the enemy in a dungeon) depends on basic common sense; yet she is convicted partly on the fact that she refuses to wear fine dresses in her situation. Joan's greatness and the turning point in this scene occur in her defiant act of tearing up her recantation. Here, Joan represents Shaw's dynamic "Life Force"—a force that cannot exist in the confinement of a dungeon hole. For Joan to live without the sky, the church bells, the fields, and, in essence, without freedom is more frightening than burning at the stake. Joan's last act of freedom is *to choose death* rather than to submit to perpetual imprisonment. And in so choosing death, Joan has set the path for her canonization and her sainthood.

EPILOGUE

Summary

The setting in this scene is King Charles's bedchamber, twenty-five years after the last scene. Charles (the former Dauphin) puts aside his book, rings for his servant, and Ladvenu enters, carrying the same cross which he held when The Maid perished at the stake. Now he announces that twenty-five years later, at the court of inquiry for rehabilitation, Joan has been declared innocent of all charges for which she was burned as a heretic. Likewise, her judges have been declared "full of corruption, cozenage, fraud, and malice." Charles, however, is not interested in The Maid, but only in removing the troublesome rumor that he was crowned by a witch and a heretic. Furthermore, he points out that were Joan to return, "they would burn her again within six months . . . so, let The Maid rest." Ladvenu, shocked at this attitude, hastily retreats.

The king again rings for his servant, but the candles go out and in a flash of lightening, a silhoutte is seen and the voice of Joan is heard. She assures Charles that he is dreaming, and she wants to know what has happened in the last twenty-five years. Charles is pleased to report that Joan forced him to become a man; he is now Charles the Victorious, and furthermore, just today, Joan has been vindicated and her judges have been condemned. Joan accepts the information without emotion, saying ironically, "They were as honest a lot of poor fools as ever burned their betters." Charles thinks The Maid should thank him for bringing about justice, but suddenly Peter Cauchon appears between them, contradicting the king. Cauchon complains bitterly of the dishonors done to him: he was excommunicated, and his body was dug up and flung into the sewer—all in order to praise Joan. Cauchon claims that he was "pure of heart" and that he was just, merciful, and faithful. King Charles merely observes that "it is always you good men that do the big mischiefs," whereas he, the king, has simply been serving France. Joan wonders then if the English are really gone, and immediately Dunois, The Bastard, appears to assure Joan that he kept his word: the English are gone. Dunois tells Joan that the French forces won by fighting by Joan's strategies, and he is sorry that he didn't come to her defense and prevent "the priests from burning her."

As the clock strikes, a rough, strange voice is heard "trolling an improvised tune," and a coarse, ruffian-like English soldier appears. He announces that he has come straight from Hell where they give him one day off each year because of one good deed which he has performed. He is about to call it "the silliest thing you ever heard of," when Joan breaks in to explain that this is the soldier who gave her two sticks tied together as a cross when she was about to be burned. The soldier then explains that Hell is not so bad – some "tip top company . . . emperors and popes and kings and all sorts" are to be found there.

Again the door opens, and an old, white-haired priest enters. It is de Stogumber, who has never recovered from witnessing Joan's burning at the stake. He now wanders around aimlessly, exhorting people to be kind to one another. When de Stogumber fails to recognize Joan because he thinks Joan is burnt and dead, the Executioner appears, announcing that Joan is more alive than de Stogumber because Joan's heart would not burn and her spirit is "up and alive everywhere." Warwick then suddenly enters to congratulate Joan on her rehabilitation and explains that the burning was nothing personal, but only a purely political necessity.

Suddenly, a stranger appears, dressed in the fashion of 1920, and therefore eliciting uncontrollable laughter from others for his comic dress. He ignores their frivolous behavior, however, and he reads from a recent proclamation that Joan The Maid has now been canonized and elevated to sainthood and that a memorial service to Saint Joan shall be celebrated every thirtieth of May, on the anniversary of her burning. Suddenly, visions of statues of Joan are seen in front of cathedrals, and all kneel to offer Joan praise; then, one by one, each of them tells of how various sectors of society praise her.

Joan interrupts their praise by reminding them that as a saint, she can effect miracles; therefore, she asks them whether or not she should come back to life as a living woman and return to them.

This very thought causes immense consternation, and with apologies and excuses, they all state that they prefer that she remain dead. Then they all slip quietly away, leaving her alone with the soldier who gave her the crude cross made of two sticks. As the soldier begins to try to comfort Joan, the stroke of midnight summons him back to Hell. As the rays of white radiant light enfold Joan, she asks God when the world will be ready to receive His saints: "How long, O Lord, how long?"

Commentary

The Epilogue takes place twenty-five years after the main events of the play and is called an Epilogue (and not Scene VII) because it exists in the world of dreams or fantasies, and it projects certain views of Joan after her death and her reactions to these events.

During the twenty-five years, actions have been underway to reverse Joan's conviction, and the scene opens on the day that the reversal has finally been accomplished. Thus, the Epilogue confirms only what the audience has long known. However, the Epilogue is encompassed by a single idea – first, King Charles VII maintains in his opening remarks that were The Maid to return to life, she would be burned again within six months. And the final closing remark of The Maid, after each person has totally rejected the idea of her reappearance, is her question: "How long, O Lord, how long?" – that is, how long will it be before the world will be ready to accept its saints (and its geniuses).

Furthermore, what is not dramatically stated but implied is the reason behind Joan's "rehabilitation." Part of the matter must be accredited to the secular arm of the nation – that is, the Dauphin was crowned by Joan, and now he has become King Charles the Victorious; consequently, it is a sore spot, a blotch on his kinghood that he received his crown from the hands of a convicted witch and a burned heretic. How much, then, the reversal of Joan's conviction was due to political expediency is not solved, but, instead, only intimated.

What is also implied in this scene is that in addition to Joan's innocence is the fact that her death *could* have been avoided. But the world is never willing to accept the distracting aspects of the saint or the genius, and only after that genius is dead does the world realize what it has rejected. Ultimately, Shaw is criticizing his own society for not accepting his own rather radical ideas, ideas that *were* radical during Shaw's time, but ideas which are now more readily accepted.

As each of the people who once praised Joan for her actions during her life now desert her when she offers to return to earth, we hear the above idea reiterated. Cauchon maintains that Joan is better off dead because, even today, "mortal eyes cannot distinguish the saint from the heretic." The others also find ways of convincing Joan to avoid returning to this world. And, finally, Joan is left alone with the English soldier, ironically the one whom she was left alone with at the stake, and he cannot fully understand her plight and, instead, he must return to Hell. Joan, then, is still alone, as she was when she spoke of the loneliness of France and the loneliness of God, in Scene Five. The final implication is that the world will never be ready to accept its saints or its geniuses.

SUGGESTED THEME TOPICS

1. Discuss in detail Shaw's view of Saint Joan. How is his view of her different in its historical context or from the way in which others have portrayed her? Does Shaw aim toward historical accuracy?

2. Once Shaw said that the first three scenes were "just theatre to get you interested – now [with Scene Four] the play begins." Discuss, first of all, what Shaw meant by "just theatre," and then discuss what he meant about Scene Four being the real beginning of the drama.

3. What possible meanings, real and ironic, could Shaw mean by entitling his play "Saint Joan"; discuss Shaw's possible views toward saints and miracles and voices.

4. Discuss what is meant by the terms "Protestantism" and "Nationalism," as used by Cauchon and Warwick. How do each of the terms threaten either the Church or the Aristocracy?

5. Discuss in detail the function of the Epilogue. Consider the play without the Epilogue and how its absence would change the nature of the play.

SELECTED BIBLIOGRAPHY

DUFFIN, H. C. *The Quintessence of Bernard Shaw*. London, 1920.

FULLER, EDMUND. *George Bernard Shaw, Critic of Western Morale*. New York, 1950.

HOWE, P. P. *Bernard Shaw*. London, 1915.

IRVINE, WILLIAM. *The Universe of GBS*. New York, 1949.

KRONENBERGER, LOUIS, ed. *George Bernard Shaw: A Critical Survey*.

MENCKEN, H. L. *George Bernard Shaw: His Plays*. Boston, 1905.

RATTRAY, R. F. *Bernard Shaw: A Chronicle and an Introduction*.

SKIMPOLE, HERBERT. *Bernard Shaw: The Man and His Work*. London, 1918.

STRAUSS, E. *Bernard Shaw, Art, and Socialism*. London, 1942.

WARD, A. C. *Bernard Shaw*. London, 1951.

NOTES

NOTES

NOTES

NOTES

NOTES

NOTES